The Arctic to Antarctica

the Arctic
to Antarctica

CIGRA CIRCUMNAVIGATES THE AMERICAS

Mladen Sutej

FineEdge.com

Credits: photos by Sutej and members of the
expedition crew, unless otherwise specified
Editor: Réanne Douglass
Copyediting: Elayne Wallis and Cindy Kamler
Map graphics: Sue Athmann
Book design: Melanie Haage Design

Library of Congress Cataloging-in-Publication Data
Sutej, Mladen, 1945–
[Na rubovima svijeta. English]
The Arctic to Antarctica : Cigra circumnavigates the Americas / by Mladen Sutej.
   p.   cm.
   ISBN 0-938665-65-0
   1. Yachting—Croatia.   2. Sutej, Mladen, 1945–   3. Sailors—Croatia—Biography.
I. Title.

GV817.C87 S8813 1999
797.1'246'092—dc21
[B]   99-045359

Address requests for permission to FineEdge.com:
13589 Clayton Lane, Anacortes, WA 98221
www.FineEdge.com

Contents

The *Arctic Tern* nests in the Arctic and winters in the Antarctic, enjoying more daylight than any other creature on earth. With a wingspan of about forty centimeters, the *Arctic Tern* is a master of flight and sailing; this small bird covers about 35,000 kilometers along the meridian routes every year apparently without effort.*

---

*Hrvatska cigra, *Croatian Tern*, was the name chosen for the expedition's 65-foot steel sailing yacht. For simplicity, we have used *Cigra* throughout the text.

The Arctic

The seeds of my nautical dream to sail the Northwest Passage were planted several years ago when Carol, my wife, and I were in Dutch Harbor, Alaska sailing back from Japan. I announced to her then that I wanted to build a boat and make the challenging journey through the Northwest Passage. By this time Carol had sailed in excess of 65,000 miles with me. She said, "Great, as long as I don't have to go." With that settled, we made it back home to Nanaimo, British Columbia, where I sold *Dove II*, and started *Dove III*. Early on, I had approached sailing instructor George Hone to ask if he would like to come with me on the trip up North. He said yes in 1991 and, in 1995, when *Dove III* was finished, he was still willing to go. Rounding out the crew was Len Sherman, a local artist, who wanted to take the trip to sketch the natives. Just prior to our departure, we had heard there was another sailboat attempting to make it through the passage from east to west, but we could not find out who it was.

Our voyage began on May 8th, 1995 as we worked our way up the Canadian coast to Dixon Entrance and the 1,200 miles across to Dutch Harbor, Alaska. We battled the weather consistently, pushing ourselves across a very rough Bering Sea to Nome, Alaska. We continued up to the Chukchi Sea, crossing the Arctic Circle at noon June 27. From there our progress slowed significantly; we were pitched into the ice many times and able to make only five to ten miles a day. We had to get around Barrow, Alaska quickly if we were to make the narrow window of opportunity north of King William Island. We sailed down to Herschel Island, around to Tuk and then completed the 600 miles to Cambridge Bay. It was there that we heard of the Croatians' boat, *Cigra*, which was caught in the ice around Bellot Strait.

We worried that the season was getting late. The ice had not yet let go, preventing us from getting to Gjøa Haven. We waited. Finally, on August 15, we saw the lights of Gjøa Haven and, on August 17 we sailed "around the corner." Len, who was at the helm, claimed to see trees on the horizon. We dashed up on deck and spotted a ketch on the horizon. We knew it must be the Croatians, and we were soon rafted up to them for what proved to be a short, but great visit.

Miro Muhek, who could speak the best English, did most of the translating. We shared information about the ice conditions in both directions, knowing that they would have to hurry to make it around Point Barrow, Alaska before the first freeze. We then said our farewells and bid goodbye to *Cigra* and her hospitable crew.

Fighting through a lot more ice, we successfully crossed the Arctic Circle, joyfully completing my dream of sailing the Northwest Passage on August 31, 1995.

Upon our return home I put together a slide show of our adventures. When I heard that the Croatian team was in Vancouver I invited them to participate in the presentation. We were able to reunite and share with the audience our various experiences of the challenges of the Northwest Passage.

The Croatians are a great bunch of guys. I understand their thoughts and share their frustrations. When you have never been in the ice, it's hard to explain the pressure you are under to accomplish a trip like this. You are constantly plagued by questions such as: Is the ice going to lock us in hundreds of miles from nowhere? Will it wreck our boat? What do we do if we have a major breakdown?

It takes a special type of person to attempt a trip like this. Those who try are all cut from the same block of wood. I hope someday to meet Mladen, Miro and their crew again. May God bless them and may the seas be kind to all who attempt this hazardous, but rewarding, journey!

Capt. Winston Bushnell
Dove III, Nanaimo, B.C.

Editor's note: Winston Bushnell and his family circumnavigated the world in their 10-meter sailboat, *Dove II*. During their crossing of the South Indian Ocean the boat was capsized in a giant wave, and they were forced to spend six months in Capetown, South Africa repairing her. His voyage through the Northwest Passage is documented in the book *Arctic Odyssey* by Len Sherman.

Antarctica

One of the most distinctive landscapes of the Beagle Channel in Southern Patagonia is the serrated sand cliff which forms the western end of Isla Gable. In stark contrast to the rest of this long, lonely seaway of wind-blasted fjords and glowering black crags, its brown, saw-toothed outline brilliantly lit in the low, setting sun has become to us a sort of beacon to signal the imminent arrival into Puerto Williams. Even here at the end of the world one has to have a place to call home, and Puerto Williams, although sometimes sadly lacking in bonhomie, was it.

After making the umpteenth stock-up trip to Ushuaia, this jagged outline had burned itself into our minds. Much of our long, downwind runs "home" were spent watching the dunes rise out of the channel, the wind pressing whoever was on the helm against the wheel in *Northanger*'s open cockpit. Seen against such a stunning backdrop, the glass fortress of *Cigra*'s pilothouse makes quite an impression, especially when the sleety rain is being hammered through the walls of your coffee cup, your fingers welded to the helm to prevent the gibe. Our *Northanger* is a pretty boat, but it is one built for suffering in the great British tradition, and it is tempting to cast aspersions on large, comfortable-looking boats from the moral high ground of the foul-weather-in-your-face club. Our curiosity was aroused by the *Cigra*, however, and once we were snugged down in Puerto Williams, we lost no time in accepting Mladen and Miro's invitation to tour their ship.

Stepping from *Northanger* into *Cigra* is like walking from a small log cabin into a spacious condo. Even though both boats purport to be designed for the same type of activity, the two boats are as divergent in design as is possible. *Northanger* was built for very small, tight expeditions with a specific goal; there is no elbow room for anything else. *Cigra*, by contrast, seemed capable of carrying mountains of equipment and a crew of all types in her cavernous and efficient interior. We secretly marveled at the comfort and visibility afforded by the vast acreage in her pilothouse. She really did seem like a boat built for the high-latitude expedition, but we left wondering whether she was too big and expensive to be capable of producing a real, meaningful journey aside from her publicity value. Talking to Mladen and Miro, however, assured us that the crew were indeed driven by strong dreams as is the blessing and curse of all such boats that pick up the gauntlet dropped by the high, cold seas of the Southern Ocean.

Our diverse vessels played a game of cat and mouse as we sailed south to Cape Horn, *Northanger* for a lengthy tryst with the mountains of the Antarctic Peninsula; *Cigra* for points south and east. Though we had had so little time to get to know the *Cigra* and her crew, the encounter left an indelible impression and I don't doubt that one day in the future we will again see that unique silhouette on one of our seagoing adventures. There will be more stories to tell that day.

Greg Landreth
Northanger

Editor's note: Canadians Greg Landreth and his wife, Keri Paschek, are co-owners of the 16-meter steel ketch, Northanger, which traversed the Northwest Passage in 1988-89. In 1995-96 they staged a first summiting of Mount Foster in the Antarctic, earning the Tilman Medal of the Royal Cruising Club of Great Britain. As this book goes to print, they are locked in Arctic ice off Ellesmere Island, supporting the Norwegian Sverdrup Centennial Expedition.

Preface

When you have completed the rather extraordinary feat of sailing around the world, all the haps and mishaps you have experienced, all the people and regions you have discovered need to be jotted down and put into book shape. I admit that this part of a voyage does not interest me a great deal, but it is pleasant to remember it all, especially what it was that led me in the first place to spend so much time on the high seas. Writing the book about my voyage to Cape Horn[1] on the sailboat *Hir 3* in 1989 and riffling through memories, I found that I had spent more than forty years on canoes and open kayaks, small sailing boats and various cruisers, as well as on my beloved *Hir*—a total of over 120,000 sea miles. So it seemed reasonable to ask myself, before this journey, whether there was any point in setting out on the oceans once again.

Rationally, there was not. It might have been better to change my way of life a little, to return to my vocation as an engineer, to devote more time to my family, and to see friends, for when I sail I find it more and more difficult to come back to land. Could it be some genetic characteristic that dragged me away from my engineering work, from the drawing board and management of business that originally made me take to the sea? I don't know, but perhaps it is because life at sea is so different, so close to nature, so close to the edge.

I return from a three-year voyage full of new experiences, images, acquaintances, and knowledge and feel I could go on for

days giving excited ac-
counts of everything I have
seen, the places I have
been. But I find that I
become confused, as if the
clock of life has stopped or
slowed so much that noth-
ing new has happened on
land while I was gone. I
realize that every remem-
bered conversation with a
new acquaintance at some
distant anchorage was a
source of great wealth, that
even an ordinary beach
stone was a valued sou-
venir, and that my friends
on land who have not
shared those experiences
do not understand my confusion.

From day to day, the rift between my land-based surroundings
and me deepens, yet that most frequent of stultifying questions—
"What are your next plans?"—does not prod me into making any
quick decisions. It is hard to give an answer that carries convic-
tion, especially if I have not yet completely come to terms with
myself. But time does work its way.

When my sailing companion, Ozren Bakrac, and I were on
Hir 3 in Ushuaia, the southernmost town in the world, we came
to know several sailors, but it was Jean-Paul, the former commander of Cousteau's *Calypso*, who made the greatest impression
on us. We never forgot his stories of the Antarctic, which at the
time was temptingly close (500 miles), yet unattainably distant.
Even then in the Beagle Channel, in the very place the Indians

called "the bay that is protected from the west winds," I imagined what it would be like to sail into the ice, the packs and mountains of Antarctica. I speculated about the cold, the regions of the unknown, about routes beyond the frontiers of reason.

It was there in Ushuaia in 1989 that a new challenge was born, one I did not dare to talk much about either to friends or acquaintances. For several years I studied the literature in peace, twirled the globe and turned over maps, thinking up various combinations. Then, because I had to start somewhere, I confided in my wife Tatjana. And, instead of suggesting I see a psychiatrist, she volunteered to design the logo[2] for the new expedition to be called—The Arctic to Antarctica.

At the first meeting in 1993, I called together nine people, intelligent folk, who had the strength and organizational abilities to come to grips with this expedition to circumnavigate North and South America. After my introductory words, there was a strange silence in the room.

But once the silence was broken, we came up with the usual reaction—that, for a project of this kind, we had neither the boat nor the money.

But for me it was a simple matter, in a way. I felt that if you don't have anything to begin with, you have nothing to lose. Why not take the chance and have a go at it? Twenty-three months later, we were to see our first icebergs in the Labrador Sea, but before then, we faced a monumental challenge.

Croatia was still in a state of war. Two years earlier, the inexorable process of the collapse of the artificial creation called Yugoslavia had begun. After 70 grim years, the ideology of communism had broken down and, with it, all unnaturally created states. But unlike some countries, such as Czechoslovakia, where the transition unfolded in a decent and humane way, evil took the upper hand in Croatia.

Serbia, the most populous of the former Yugoslav state, had

the majority of the army, police and arms under its control. It was organized for war and unwilling to accept the collapse of a system from which it profitted. Slovenia extricated itself from the situation with a seven-day war, but fate reserved a worse outcome for Croatia. War took hold of our country and lasted, with varying degrees of intensity, for five years.

Now, in a country that had been at war with Serbia for two

years, I needed to hold a press conference, to go public with our plan for sailing around the world from north to south—the longitudinal route. I was terrified. How would people react to a project of this kind? At a time when arms purchases were more important than anything else, here was a group of people planning an incredible, crazy voyage around the world—and an expensive one at that.

Fortunately, my fears were unfounded. Instead of attacking me, people were sympathetic to the whole idea. Something new had appeared on the dismal horizon of a life filled with conditions we never imagined could be repeated, not in this day and age, and in the middle of Europe. Ours was an outrageous kind of idea involving a group of people who didn't seem to care about the war.

The manager of a big advertising agency said: "I have to hand it to you. This is the best thing Croatia has to offer at the present time. You're showing the world that there are other things going on in this country apart from the dirty war we have been dragged into."

While Croatia was still at war, my group conceived the project, assembled the necessary money and assistance, built the boat, and set off on the voyage. During one of the last discussions about the composition of the crew, when *Cigra* was already in Canadian winter quarters, eight bombs fell on Zagreb, the capital of Croatia where I live, the city from which the whole project was being run. One of the bombs almost killed my secretary at the entrance to a bank; a second fell a few hundred meters from the cafe where I was holding a meeting. Here in the city with a population of about one million, air-raid sirens would wail every so often; there were corpses on the streets, in dwellings, and on the battlefield. My associates and I regularly spent hours in various air raid shelters while enemy planes flew overhead.

In this strange and unnatural atmosphere, a spirit of defiance and resistance developed, a will to succeed, accompanied by extraordinary enthusiasm and readiness to make all kinds of sacrifices, not only within our own team but many other people as well. Our project went ahead with unimaginable speed.

Ironically, it was the shipyard in Kraljevica,[3] one that had built naval vessels throughout its 270-year history, that offered to construct the yacht. From the first days of war with Serbia, this shipyard had been targeted because it was building a modern and expensively-equipped ship that the Serbs wanted. When they failed to get hold of it, and when the Croatian flag was raised on the warship, enemy planes attacked the shipyard. By chance, our boat *Cigra,* was built in the same shed as the military ship and could well have been destroyed before it was launched.

The main office of our project, the Arctic-Antarctica Expedition, was set up in Zagreb, not only because most of us lived in the city, but also because many of our friends and most of the larger firms we had asked for help and sponsorship were located there. Then, when construction of the yacht began, about 15 of our expedition members moved to Kraljevica where we rented a house to live in to be able to work on the project. I spent half the week in Zagreb trying to raise money and the second half in Kraljevica organizing the work.

Not quite three months after our first public meeting, the project team had 30 members. Two months later, as many as 150 people were involved—all were volunteers who did not receive a penny for their time and efforts.

Of the companies we asked for help, the first to respond was the shipyard. They wanted to prove that they were capable of building a steel yacht, the first ever in their history, that they had the know-how and technology for dealing with thin plate. As the manager of the yard, Mr. Walter, himself an engineer, said, "There is not such a great difference between a naval vessel and a sailing yacht. Both must be fast, which means they must be lightweight; both need thin plating."

The shipyard in Kraljevica became not only our chief sponsor but also the prime mover of our expedition, because all the money, equipment, and documentation had to keep pace with the tempo of their work.

As always in such undertakings, money was the chief obstacle. It was easier to obtain metal plating, plywood, insulation material, and other items produced inside Croatia than to raise money. Unfortunately, sails, masts, deck gear, engines, pumps, and electronics are not manufactured in Croatia, and foreign manufacturers did not show any great desire to sponsor us. Thus the solution was to raise money in Croatia and to buy equipment outside. Since this was my third expedition on the world's seas, I had had a lot of experience in finding backers, and I was respected in Croatia. As a qualified engineer, I had friends and colleagues in all the most important firms. As a long-time yachtsman, I had credibility with sporting and nautical institutions.

Many of the people taking part in the project doubted whether we could manage to get enough backers to finance the boat, but I did not share their pessimism. For years I have claimed that, on the whole, the problem lies not in money but in ideas. Funds did exist, even in a disabled and wounded Croatia, but there is always a shortage of real ideas and of people who *can* and *will* put them into action. Little by little, 115 companies became involved in the project; they helped in building and fitting out the yacht, procuring sails and provisions, and in providing funds for the voyage.

Donations and support of firms from abroad were small compared to those of Croatia, and the project was realized almost entirely on home ground. The great majority of sponsors asked for no favors in return for the money they contributed. For many people the building of *Cigra* was a matter of prestige and national honor. Everyone wanted to show that Croatia, although a small country and one in considerable difficulty, was capable of putting together and carrying through a positive, ambitious project such as this.

When the voyage was over, we gave most of our sponsors good photographs, video material, and a score of postcards from places around the world. That was all. INA, the Croatian petroleum company, and one of the main sponsors of the expedition, certainly did not increase its sales because of its advertisement on our sails, but many of its employees must have been happy to see the company's logo at Cape Horn and sailing across Drake Passage. The whole of Croatia has seen the 13 half-hour video series about *Cigra*'s voyage at least once.

The members of the crew, 37 in all, who took part in the three-year voyage, were selected according to certain criteria. The most important was to have been with us in the preparatory phase and during construction of the boat. Most of us had quit our jobs and were neglecting responsibilities to our families. We all worked for two years, without a break, without weekends off, until *Cigra* at last touched the sea. These were the people who most deserved to sail around the world. Not a single member of the crew paid or bought his way in; hard work and support of the project were the only qualifications.

Setting off from Croatia, I was certain the expedition would be a success. The people I had the honor to command were a terrific crew, most of them people with university degrees, who had put their brains, know-how, energy, and enthusiasm into the project. If there was any justice in the world, we would succeed in our ideals and goals because of their devotion. Choosing the crew was not difficult. For many years, I have run a sailing school, teaching sailing and navigation to more than 1,600 people. With all of them, I have lived onboard small craft, sailed in rain and snow, cooked on mountaineering stoves, and slept in wet sleeping bags. I knew these people well and chose the best of them.[4]

We set out from Croatia in May, 1994 and, in that same year on our shake-down cruise, we saw icebergs in the Labrador Sea. A year later, we were breaking through the ice in Prince Regent Inlet in the Arctic as the Croatian army scattered the remnants of the Serb army and liberated the remaining 20 percent of occupied land. The war had ended. It was a fitting beginning to our Northwest Passage.

---

1. *Jedrilicom Oko Cape Horna,* Zagreb 1991.

2. Tanja's logo which shows a bird gradually turning into a sailboat appears on page i.

3. The seaport of Kraljevica is about 175 kilometers (108 miles) southwest of Zagreb, on the Adriatic. The shipyard where *Cigra* was built has specialized in the construction of large military vessels since the 18th Century.

4. A list of the crew members appears in the Appendix.

One year pack ice in Baffin Bay; about a half-meter thick, it rises only about an inch above the surface. The puddles are formed when ice melts above the surface of the water

chapter one

Into the Fog

Before we sailed out of St. John's, Newfoundland, for our shakedown cruise in 1994, I had visited the Canadian Coast Guard which controls all voyages within its territorial waters—vast portions of the Atlantic and Pacific oceans, as well as the Arctic. Due to their magnitude, Canadian waters rank number two in size worldwide, and these expanses are difficult to imagine, let alone to monitor.

The Canadian Coast Guard is a civilian establishment, which is a big difference from similar organizations in the United States or South America. When the Canadians intercept or inspect you, weapons are not evident, as is the case with their southern neighbors.

Following the tragedy of the passenger liner *Titanic*, an organization called the International Ice Patrol was established. With all the means now at its disposal—planes, satellites, boats and other equipment—the Patrol attempts to register and predict the path of every sizeable piece of floating ice in the waters of the North Atlantic, especially in the Labrador Sea, the most dangerous zone of all.

I was interested in the zone around Newfoundland and the Canadian north to Greenland and the Arctic and asked the Coast Guard for all the data they had about the ice situation and for the frequencies on which we could receive or send information. The ice chart showed four icebergs in various positions, 50 to 180 miles north of Newfoundland, and packs of them some 600 miles farther north, between Labrador and Greenland. Their evaluation was that, at the beginning, with a course that would take us a bit to the east and then with a heading of 010° we shouldn't encounter any problems.

I wondered if they had managed to register all the really important dangers. We knew, for example, that growlers[1] cannot be seen from the air or detected even by satellite. But it is hard to predict everything, nor would there be the same excitement if every detail were known in advance. So with this meager information we set out on our voyage to Greenland, 850 miles away, and the largest island in the world. To new realms of ice, to the fogs in abundance, to something completely unknown.

Very soon we had to put on the warm boots and multi-layered clothing that we had bought in Canada. Summer daytime temperatures fell to 10°C (50°F) and, at night, the mercury hit zero (32°F). Everything was drenched in the fog and rain that are the main features of this zone. The numerous books and pilots about the area—once known for its exceptionally heavy fishing and marine traffic—regularly begin with warnings about the fog, which, combined with rapid cyclonic alterations, heavy seas and ice, has caused countless wrecks and collisions at sea. The fog around Newfoundland is created by the encounter of two currents: the warm Gulf Stream that flows up the eastern seaboard of the U.S. which, north of 40° N heads off toward Europe, and the

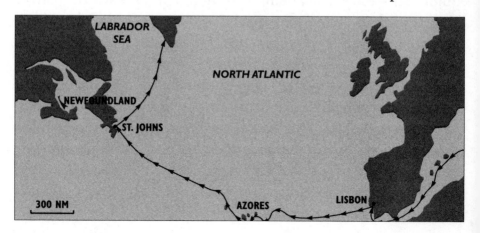

We caught sight of our first iceberg, magnificent, beautiful and terrifying

cold Labrador Current that flows southward from the Arctic Ocean. The current also brings with it icebergs that break off the great Greenland icecap. The marine currents are accompanied by air currents, and when they mingle, thick fog is created, so dense that sometimes not even the powerful westerlies can disperse it.

In such sailing conditions, apart from the usual methods of monitoring the situation at sea and the watchfulness of every conscientious sailor, radar is the most gratifying piece of equipment. Although it sends some people to sleep faster than does their bed, it does show ships here and there, as well as a wandering piece of ice in the Newfoundland zone.

The radar on *Cigra* was particularly important, because the windows of our large, safe and specially-designed wheelhouse were constantly fogged up by rain or 100% humidity. Add to this, during periods of low temperatures, the innate fondness of the crew for dishes like beans and sausages and long-simmered stews, there was no chance of seeing even the bow of the boat through the window, let alone twenty meters beyond.

The night watch crew lessened visibility even further by making tea or mulling wine, and sailing became a completely blind, instrument-guided ride in which radar—as long as there was battery power—was the main entertainment of those on the bridge. Everyone knows that part of the ice, particularly the growlers, don't show up on radar. Nevertheless, human optimism led those who were sleeping to hope that the antenna was turning and that the helmsman was going to notice every ice cube.

With the westerlies and southwesterlies, we made quick progress northwards. On our fourth day out, we sighted our first iceberg to port, and a second a few hours later. I caught my breath at the sight of this magnificent, beautiful and terrifying sight. Srecko made a sketch of the ice monsters in *Cigra's* log, making note of their approximate dimensions.

At 0400, the radar warned of a new encounter with the ice when we were just 35 miles off Cape Farewell, the southernmost point of Greenland. I was already beginning to worry why we hadn't encountered ice earlier, since the *Admiralty Pilot* says the first ice in these waters ought to be seen 80 miles from the Cape.

After that and, for almost a year later, when we were once again underway following a similar route along the coast of Greenland, ice, icefloes, and icebergs, all the derivations of the word, *ice,* took on an everyday familiarity.

Now, less and less frequently we heard the clicking of cameras, and the crew stopped exclaiming over every berg. Comparisons such as "This one looks like a fountain . . . That one is like a huge armchair . . . Look! That one is as big as a cathedral . . ." slowly died out. We no longer estimated the height of the icebergs, except when we were in their immediate vicinity and our 20-meter mast could serve as a direct comparison.

Having become somewhat accustomed to the ice, we began to draw closer to it, and sometimes it would approach us. The knowledge that the average iceberg shows only 12 percent of its beauty above the surface, and that the rest of its thousands of tons of mass lies submerged, hundreds of meters deep, is not exactly

We began to draw closer to the icebergs

encouraging. But there is no point in speculating what would happen if one of these great blocks were to knock us about; time is better spent calculating the speed and direction of its movement and the influence of the wind and the current.

That first year in Greenland though, we did miss out on something: we managed to avoid making the acquaintance of our most

The Greenland icecap which stretches the entire length of the island is the second biggest slab of ice on Earth (after the Antarctic) and the source of many of the icebergs and growlers we encountered

In Narrsaq Sund, Greenland, 61° N, night lasts just a few hours in summer

dangerous future enemy—not the bergs, not even the treacherous growlers, but the frozen surface of the sea, the thin, one-year crust called pack ice.[2]

I never did manage to make friends with the ice. Every day I spent in its company I had to make an agonizing decision I was never completely sure of. To this day, I consider ice at sea a mean, nasty adversary, difficult to understand. Ice-scapes are at their best seen in photographs or viewed from the air flying over Greenland between Europe and North America. A live-encounter with the ice is a completely different story. However, long-term companionship brought us closer together . . . to the borders of tolerant respect.

1. Growlers are parts of icebergs that have split into thousands of pieces. Each one may be a meter in height and 20 square meters in area; they may appear transparent, but often they are greenish or black.

2. Pack ice, the frozen surface of the sea, attains a thickness of 2 to 3 meters in winter. It stops the movement of a ship and is a danger to the hull, rudder and propeller. If you manage to break through it, the pack can close behind the boat with unimaginable speed, constantly threatening imprisonment. The word "pack" became the most despised expression on board *Cigra*.

chapter two

Shake-down and Refuge

The approach to Greenland from the Labrador Sea is theoretically quite simple. The island, which rises to 3,000 meters in elevation, is covered in ice and snow and is visible from a great distance. The first European to see it—the enterprising killer Eric the Red—described it from a distance of 50 miles. When this ruthless bandit was exiled from his native Iceland for a period of three years, instead of sailing off toward Norway, like most such offenders, he turned his bow to the west.

Eric didn't realize how lucky he was to encounter good weather and visibility. Greenland, in its full glory just a few days of the year, is usually shrouded in low cloud and fog. During his voyage, perhaps Eric was affected by the sun and strong winds, because the gray and black rock and white snow appeared green to him, causing him to name the island as he did. Or perhaps the climate of Greenland was totally different ten centuries ago. We have no way of knowing.

We sailed into the fishing village of Qaqortog with the help of our depth meter and GPS[1] and were unable to see the pier until we were just 80 meters away. We managed a radio link with the harbor authorities, which gave us soothing confirmation of the accuracy of our navigation. We were happy to know we were not actually off the coast of Iceland! We did the rest as if someone had completely blindfolded us and, while we remained in these waters a dozen days, we saw the high peaks of Greenland only twice.

Qaqortog has about 2,000 residents who earn their living hunting whale and seals, but they prefer sledding to fishing!

During the good weather we had an exceptional flight in our hang-glider.[2] The island, with its unique shapes and many-colored houses scattered over the shining landscape, made a powerful impression on us from the air, as did Norde Sermilik fjord.

During our shake-down cruise to Greenland, we learned a valuable lesson: that neither *Cigra* nor its crew would have been prepared for the voyage through the Northwest Passage that first summer. Our equipment was incomplete; there was too much that was new and untested and we had not run all the systems enough to know how much and what the boat could stand.

Despite my visit to the Canadian Coast Guard in St. John's, we still did not have permission from the Canadian authorities. In the planning stages, before we cast off from Croatia for northern waters, we had known that we would need additional equipment as well as permission from the Canadian authorities. Our decision to postpone the Arctic voyage until the next year was not made at the last minute; we had known that we would have to find accommodations for both *Cigra* and the crew for the winter of 1994-5. However, we still did not know where we were going to winter.

We quickly discovered that there was no place for us in Greenland; the shipyards were too expensive and their equipment too modest. Apart from the astronomical prices, weather conditions didn't even allow painting the hull. The other possibility—heading to Norway—was rejected, again due to steep prices. Thus, we had no alternative but to head back to Canada.

The climate in the Labrador Sea takes a sudden turn for the worse in August when there are twice as many storms as in May and June. The coast of Labrador, itself, enters a long foggy period and the sea begins to freeze over as early as the end of September. It was time to think about returning to Canada. We made use of our days in Greenland waters to check the radar, the depth meter, the pilothouse ventilation, the boat's furnace, the oil

The motorized hang-glider taking off

filters, the cleaning and de-icing devices, the windshield wipers, and our clothing. Several times we deliberately ran the bow into the ice, shoving the bergs first with the bow, then with the stern, all the time checking the sensitivity of the helm and the resistance of the bearings and hydraulics to shocks and temperature—experiments during

which we gathered a lot of useful data.

Before leaving Greenland, we made several panoramic flights in the hang-glider to an elevation of 800 meters, visited the Unartgo Fjord, and treated ourselves to a bath in the thermal spring on the island of Igpi.

If you haven't caught cold from flying high in a hang-glider or from icy drafts in an open pool, you deserve another go at the gray mass someone ironically named the Labrador Sea.[3]

Norde Sermilik fjord from a height of 500 meters (1,600 feet); the Greenland ice-cap is visible in the distance

An abandoned whale blubber processing plant, Hawkes Harbour, Labrador

Setting southwest from Greenland is best planned after a strong low-pressure front has passed and while the air temperature is essentially the same as that of the sea. Our first four days were not bad; then came the unavoidable.

We tried baking seal ribs, the local "delicacy," and found them worse than we had imagined. Some of the crew sought consolation over the rail

On August 15, we encountered southeast winds of 20 to 25 knots and fog with visibility below 100 meters. During the night, the wind veered to the southwest, hitting us straight on the bow, and "settling" at about 45 knots—conditions that lasted about 60 hours. The wind then grew even stronger so we were forced to return to our last-known position.

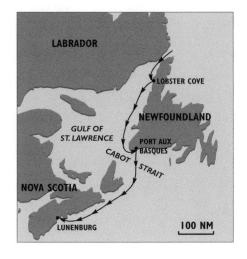

When the weather had calmed down a little, I decided to look for shelter along the closest land—Labrador. It was a good idea, but one without foundation, because we didn't have a nautical chart of the area, and I hadn't even been able to find one before we left St. John's. Using the descriptions in the British *Pilot,* we undertook the demanding and lengthy business of drawing our own map from its descriptions.

We soon tested our mapmaking skills. Fifteen miles from the coast we were able to recognize all the essential features as if we had been in home waters. But then began a new set of troubles: both the main and auxiliary engines gave up. Six days of powerful rolling and water pouring over the length of the entire hull was enough to fill both exhaust pipes with sea water. Extremely low temperatures and a cold engine room had accelerated growth of algae in the fuel tanks, and the fuel filters were filled with some kind of amorphous mass. Once again, it had been demonstrated that we were not ready to attempt the Northwest Passage.

Just when I was beginning to think that our cartographic pains had been in vain and that we would have to continue under sail, the engines—under Miro's strict supervision—began to show signs of life. But that was not our only problem. In a storm, the sea had swept a line overboard which firmly wrapped itself around the propeller.

Srecko saved us. He suited up and dove into the cold, turbulent water. In constant danger of being hit by the hull or rudder, he managed to cut the line; but from this time on, I began to consider how we might stop the shaft and screw from rotating while we were sailing.

The Strait of Belle Isle between Labrador and the north coast of Newfoundland is an important navigational route. Forty miles long and 12 miles wide, it is an unpleasant route, foggy and crowded with ships. The powerful currents created by the mixing of sea water from the Gulf of St. Lawrence and the Atlantic are particularly dangerous. Nevertheless, I was not sorry we had decided to round the west coast of Newfoundland from the north. The water of the strait seethes with local "bathers" that create a mighty jam: we saw 40 or more whales together, not to mention dolphins, seals and hundreds of species of birds. The crew of *Cigra* almost went out of its mind at such scenes.

Branimir, who works at Halifax University, Nova Scotia, had the duty of monitoring the birds (which he did conscientiously whenever he wasn't having to battle seasickness). He taught us about the colorings of birds' plumage, the shapes of their beaks, about their flight patterns, about they way they dive into the crest of a wave with a single wing, and about the various kinds of mischief perpetrated by gannets, ducks, shearwaters.

But in the Strait of Belle Isle there was too much material even for Branimir. With birds fluttering around the mast, he didn't know which way to turn. Photographing with his long lens, he quite often collided with Jelena, who was in charge of diving, observing the mammals, and collecting samples of the benthos (organisms that live on the seafloor). During night watches, Jelena would often play cassettes of dolphin calls, hoping to attract them to the boat, but it usually had the opposite effect.

Each lobster pot has a plastic ring with a number and the name of its owner; any fisherman found with an unmarked pot must pay a fine of $1000.

Now, not even this method dispersed the mass of marine mammals in the Strait of Belle Isle. The whales came to within 10 meters of *Cigra*, hailing us by raising their tail fins and giving us a cold shower, a show that lasted for hours. When darkness fell we found shelter in Lobster Cove, and the next day, as we continued south along the coast of Newfoundland we called at Gros Morne National Park[4] which gave us a pleasant contrast from the sea.

Although it may seem strange to a mariner, there is almost no yachting on the Atlantic side of Canada; the climate and temperamental ocean do their work. In the port of Halifax, on Nova Scotia's west coast, and even in Lake Ontario you find few yacht

Crabs destined for Japan are caught at a depth of more than 100 meters (328 feet).

Gros Morne National Park on the west coast of Newfoundland gave us a pleasant change from the blue of the sea

clubs and marinas. So, to our questions about where we could tie up a 20-meter boat and await the end of the cold winter, we received only shrugs of the shoulders.

A little town of 2,000 inhabitants with a German name came as the only solution. We sailed southwest from Halifax and into the port of Lunenburg one Sunday afternoon, not knowing that we had put into one of the Canada's greatest tourist attractions, a former fishing center that holds safe anchorage for 50 fishing schooners, a marine museum, the country's oldest shipyard, and the maritime pride of Canada—the schooner *Bluenose II*.[5] Lunenburg is a famous town and, like our own Dubrovnik, has been taken under the protection of UNESCO. Let us hope it never has to suffer the same fate as our Croatian city.

Thus ended our shake-down cruise, and the first year of our expedition. Miro and Dubravko remained in Lunenburg to look after *Cigra,* pursuing odd jobs in the meantime. Srecko flew home to check out the situation at his university, and Jelena went home to her parents in Toronto. Tanja and I returned to Zagreb and set about preparing for the next stage of the voyage.

---

1. GPS (Global Positioning System) was developed by the Americans for determining accurate position and velocity based on data received from a minimum of three satellites out of two dozen in orbit. GPS is not affected by most weather, and it provided us with coverage in the high latitudes of both hemispheres, as well as in the equatorial regions. When we received a 4-satellite, 3-dimensional fix, the errors in our position were less than 150 meters, and they were calculated every 1.5 to 2 seconds.

2. Although Greenland is a good place for flying since it has a lot of windless days, the hang-glider, itself, is not practical for scouting out a navigable route through the Arctic. It takes too long to assemble and needs space to take off in. Most large Arctic vessels carry a helicopter for the job.

3. The Labrador Sea takes its name from the brilliantly colored rock on the Labrador Peninsula.

4. Although the highest point in Gros Morne Park is only 472 meters, it has some of the best ski-tracks in Eastern Canada.

5. *Bluenose II* is a faithful copy of its famous predecessor and a big attraction of Lunenburg. The fishing schooner is 49 meters long on deck, 38 meters on the waterline with a width of 9 meters and a draft of 5.1. From the deck to the top of the mast it is 42 meters. The vessel has 29 halyards and carried 10 dories for a crew of about thirty.

chapter three

Underway to the Arctic

We sailed into Nuuk, Greenland, May 1995 without sighting the coast. At the last minute, a mere three miles from the village, the first small islands appeared, then a lighthouse to starboard, and a gray mainland. We turned into a small bay and stayed there for twenty minutes without anchoring, just long enough to catch five large codfish. After the 1,100-mile voyage from St. John's, everyone could do with some fresh food.

And so began the second year of our expedition. *Cigra* had spent seven months on land in Lunenburg at the L.I.F.E. shipyard, and before the continuation of the voyage she had acquired a lot of new equipment, and an odd addition to her hull—deflectors. During the building of *Cigra* in Kraljevica, the hull technologist, Mr. Jura Crnkovic, had made a horizontal fin for deflecting the ice, and his idea took the

Lifting *Cigra* wasn't easy for even a 70-ton crane

17

sors in Lunenburg.
They suggested that
instead of *one* pair of
deflectors we should
have *three,* and these
additions very likely
saved us from disaster.
   We bought provi-
sions in Lunenburg
and a lot more came
by plane from Croatia.

Cigra spent the winter on shore hooked to the marina's electricity to keep her heated and her batteries charged

We loaded *Cigra* with about
1600 kilos of food. If Canadian
Customs had known how much
salami and prosciutto we
brought into a country where
this is tantamount to a crime,
we would not have seen Greenland a second time! But everything came off well thanks to
Miro who used his charm to
win over the young lady serving
as the local Customs officer.
   Nevertheless, it had not
been easy to leave Canada for,
until the very last day, the
authorities refused to give permission for our voyage through
the Northwest Passage. Passing
through the Canadian part of
the Arctic is complex, dangerous and almost impossible.

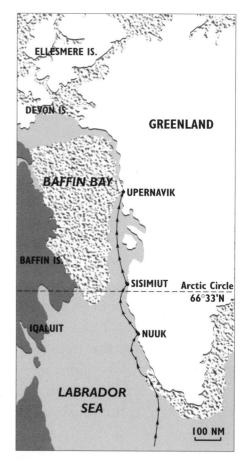

Every vessel that sets off into these waters finds itself in trouble sooner or later, and help can be expected only from the good Lord or the Coast Guard. Assistance, if it can be mounted at all, is extremely costly and difficult, so the Canadians are wary of letting ships into a danger zone where they have to foot the bill. We had negotiated with them for a full two years and, in the end, just when we thought everything was settled, they refused their permission.

At that moment, if we had not already bought warm clothing and everything else we needed for the Arctic, we might have headed for the Caribbean; but, as it was, we had nothing else to do but put up stiff resistance.

The Governor of the province of Nova Scotia, where our host town Lunenburg was located, was also the personal representative of Britain's Queen Elizabeth II. Over lunch—lasagna, lettuce salad without dressing, and cold water—he explained to Miro and me that he wouldn't pay too much attention to his own government.

"It's just bureaucratic nonsense," he said. Nevertheless, he picked up the telephone and called the Queen's secretary in London.

"It's simpler for me to explain things to Buckingham Palace than to Ottawa."

The owner of L.I.F.E. shipyard was also hopping mad. "The morons! Who do we pay our taxes to? Tell them I have written you

Relaunching *Cigra:* the horizontal fins protect the propeller from ice; the little snout on the transom is a useful addition similar to a device on an icebreaker

as..ing you to go to the Arctic to test the functioning of the deflectors we fitted around the boat's propeller. Please write me a detailed account of how well they worked out," he told me.

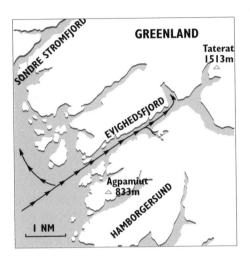

"I'll give you your fee in advance, to the tune of one silver dollar, because I know you'll do a decent job of it. I'd like to see if our government can forbid you to do something for a Canadian company!"

The Croatian Consul in Ottawa, who had become personally involved in our dilemma, was also perplexed by the stance of the Canadian Foreign Office; he got into his car and drove to the other side of the city to lodge a protest. In the meantime, we sailed northward from Nova Scotia. We mounted the silver dollar—cast with Lunenburg's symbol—on the bulkhead of *Cigra*'s salon. Permission from Ottawa caught up with us in Newfoundland, but we shall never know who deserves the credit.

Nuuk, in the Greenlandic language (Gothaab in Danish), is the largest town on the island. A fifth of the entire population of 55,000 lives there. For us, the most important person in the little town was the harbormaster, Eric Moller, the manager of the Arctic Line Company that has the concession for marine transportation, ports, and the responsibility of supplying Greenland by sea. Eric is a Dane, of course, and apart from being harbormaster and one of the most important people in Greenland, he is quite a character, a sailor who has managed to stick it out 12 years in this frigid country. When some antediluvian wooden sailing ship went down in Nuuk harbor, he bought it, raised it, put it in order and set off right into the Northwest Passage. He got no farther than Resolute, and his whole story is so amusing and witty that we laughed uproariously for months over his adventures.

But when you see his boat the *Kivioq,* you want to cry. Built for the well-known Greenland explorer, Knud Rasmussen, who headed north in search of Thule, the boat now

Diesel for the Arctic was stowed all over *Cigra*

looks so pathetic you wouldn't dare sail it even to the end of the pier.

Looking lovingly at his ship, Eric said calmly: "In just another three months I'm going to retire. Then I'll sail back home to Denmark with her."

Our friend made a big effort to make our stay pleasant and effective. He organized the supply of the highest quality fuel that Denmark could offer us, and we left Nuuk looking more like a tanker than a yacht, ready to explode sky high at any moment.

Every spare bit of space—under the table, the bunks and the settees, and all over the deck— was crammed with 4,200 liters of Arctic diesel oil, 400 liters of petrol, 800 liters of kerosene, 100 liters of light paraffin, 160 liters of various kinds of engine oil, 40 liters of fuel additive, 80 kilograms of propane gas for cooking and . . . 4,000 matches, 1,000 candles, 30 kilograms of various kinds of ammunition and lots

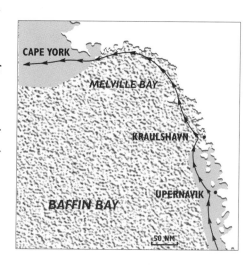

Helicopter is the main means of transportation during the Greenlandic summer, so getting to the airport is a costly business!

more trifles that in some unlucky combination could result in a display of real fireworks.

As we set off from Nuuk, Moller called to us from shore: "Good luck! You look just crazy enough to succeed."

It took us two whole days to cross the Arctic Circle, the "line" at 66°33' N latitude, not because some great wall of ice stood in our way, but because powerful north winds completely stopped our progress at one moment. When the teak planks on the bowsprit began to groan and crack, I decided to turn around and sail some 18 miles back to a fjord called No Name.

The following day, the weather improved a bit, and we toasted our arrival in Sisimiut, where Igor had booked a helicopter flight to the airport. So now, we were left without one of the best and most self-sacrificing members of our

Eskimo huskies are still irreplaceable, although motorized sleds are on the increase. These dogs are handsome but dangerous; before our arrival in Upernavik they mauled to death a little girl who slipped and fell in their midst

The sun did not set below the horizon and, when it was at its lowest point we could use it for orientation since it pointed directly north (This time-lapsed shot was taken every 30 minutes with a tripod-mounted camera)

club, whom family obligations had called back to Zagreb. I didn't attempt to persuade him to stay, because several months earlier we had agreed on his departure date.

The nights were gradually disappearing and, around two in the morning, the helmsman would grasp for his climber's sun-goggles. At these latitudes, the sun does not drop below the horizon in the west but continues its course towards the north, dropping close to the sea and shining right in your eyes. For several days I acted as if it didn't bother me, but when my eyelids began to flutter uncontrollably and my eyes filled painfully with tears, I had no alternative but to put clip-ons over my regular glasses.

North to south, Greenland is about 1,100 miles long and, from beginning to end, a vessel is in constant contact with the ice. At times there is less of it, but it is always there, confirmed by the ice charts we received via fax.

The region is covered by both Canada and Denmark, which monitor it with the same systems but with different results. The Danes' base at the airport at Narsarsuaq in the south of Greenland, was one of the most important Allied military bases during World War II. Data is gathered here by American satellites, and ice observers—trained people who, from helicopters or special ice patrol planes—provide the best and most reliable data. The information is then computer-analyzed, drawn on charts and, with a delay of some 10 to 15 hours, broadcast from Copenhagen.

The Canadian system does something similar, but much more thoroughly and for a wider area. Their main base is at Iqualit on Baffin Island; their center is in Ottawa. When we received a weather fax, we began our own analysis of conditions, always a rather complex procedure because the charts were never completely legible. The most important information is shown graphically in an oval shape which everyone in the Arctic calls "eggs." The egg has several numbers on it: the uppermost shows the concentration of ice (7–8 means that 70 to 80 percent of the sea is covered in ice); the numbers in the center indicate the type of ice; the numbers at the bottom of the egg show the size of individual floes.

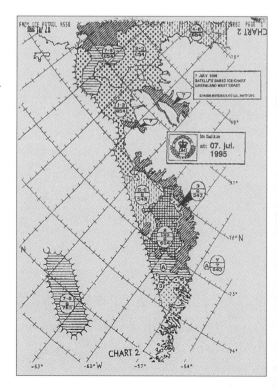

We were expecting the greatest problem in Melville Bay during the first part of the voyage through the Northwest Passage which officially began

Children in the village of Kraulshaven, 74°N[1]

when we crossed the Arctic Circle. This area, northeast of Baffin Bay, is about 160 miles long. According to the few people who have ventured into these icy waters, it is a trying experience for any vessel. The area contains masses of icebergs and ice islands whose sizes are measured in kilometers.

The great ice floes that drop into the sea from the Greenland glaciers are the consequence of precipitation and climatic conditions thousands and thousands of years old. The ice which is, on average, 10,000 to 12,000 years old, is dense, clean and good for adding to 12-year-old alcoholic beverages.

These icy monsters, which weigh thousands and thousands of tons, are poor and indolent swimmers. It takes them

Seals are the mainstay of the Eskimo diet

Calculation: if our mast is 21 meters (69 ft.) high, the iceberg is 35 (115 ft.), meaning that about 315 meters (1,033 ft.) of ice are hidden below the surface

about three years to travel from Greenland to the vicinity of Newfoundland. And there, when they suddenly find themselves in the warm Gulf Stream, they lose their "head" completely and melt in a few days. Every glacier sliding down off Greenland brings with it small quantities of stone and sand which, during the melting process, sink to a depth of 2,500 meters (8,200 ft.) at the bottom of the ocean. This long-term glacial dumping has created the famed Grand Banks off Newfoundland, a

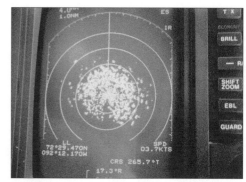

A sorry sight—*Cigra* in the center of an ice floe. The radar which can see conditions within a radius of 2 kilometers only cannot be used for planning the route

shallows only 30 to 80 meters deep that covers an expanse of about 300 miles—an area about the size of five Adriatic seas.

These floes are not the biggest barrier. The real trouble, called pack ice, is something entirely different; it is ice that has formed during the winter from the freezing of the surface of the sea. Depending on its location in the Arctic, it can attain a thickness from 1.5 to 2.5 meters (5 to 8 feet). But when the summer sun starts to shine, heating the ice a merciless 24 hours a day, the layer of ice begins to thaw and get thinner, melting completely away in some areas. Pack ice is not only useless for drinking, it is a dangerous enemy of every ship; no matter its thickness, it is often a serious obstacle even to icebreakers. Avoiding the icebergs that float mainly on their own is not difficult; the greatest navigational problem in the Arctic is how to locate and push through the hundreds and thousands of square kilometers of frozen sea.

There is another essential difference between glacier ice and pack ice. Because of their great mass, the bergs float deep in the water and are moved mainly by currents. Pack ice is much less

Caves like this in a glacier are not unusual

Moment of decision—to push through , wait or turn back?

subject to the movements of the sea, but far more influenced by the winds. This knowledge is not only essential for the safety of navigating in the Arctic, but also because it is precisely the difference in the way the ice moves that often creates a crucial opportunity to get through.

We suffered through Melville Bay for 11 days and nights. Our best results occurred when, during a 24-hour period without a stop, we covered a mile and a half! Learning a lesson from this, we began to take regular forced breaks in the ice; once for 15 hours, a second time for 28 hours, then another for 14 hours. At the beginning, naïve and inexperienced, we struck pitons into the ice and tied up to them. Later, we simplified the maneuver a bit—we just rammed the bow into pack ice and let it stay there.

If our GPS device had had a plotter and a disk to make a permanent register of the route of our wanderings, turnings, goings-back and all other kinds of maneuvers, it would have shown a curve of unimaginable shape about 800 miles long.

---

1. Hygiene is a serious problem in this village; of the 200 inhabitants, 80 had tuberculosis.

chapter four

The Pleasure of Polynya

The modern history of the Arctic begins some time at the end of the 15th century, immediately after Columbus, when a Venetian with the unlikely name of John Cabot (and immediately afterward his son Sebastian) sought a different, shorter route to China. The Cabots were followed by the Frenchman, Cartier, who had two Croats in his crew, and then by Martin Frobisher, an Englishman. They were all trying to carry on from where Pytheas, the Greek, had left off, setting sail from Marseilles to the frozen north 2,300 years earlier in search of amber.

What these maritime successors of Pytheas were looking for later gained an official name: the Northwest Passage. But the existence of such a passage through the Arctic region was proved only at the beginning of the Twentieth Century by the Norwegian explorer Roald Amundsen.

One of the most courageous men to have marked the 20th Century, Amundsen began preparing himself for his polar triumphs as a young man by skiing, exercising to build up his strength, and sleeping with windows open in the winter. He set out from Norway in 1903 in the 47-ton sailing vessel, *Gjøa*, to explore the Northwest Passage and to make observations at the North Magnetic Pole. *Gjøa* was caught in ice for two seasons, and Amundsen and his crew carried out their observations and explorations until the season of 1905 when they successfully completed the Northwest Passage.

Since that time, a fairly precise definition of the Northwest
Passage has been developed. The Canadian *Pilot* describes it as
follows:

> *The Northwest Passage spans the North American Arctic from Davis
> Strait and Baffin Bay in the east to Bering Strait in the west, and has
> four potentially feasible routes.*[1]

Despite the existence of four possible routes through the Arctic,
there is really only one unless you have an icebreaker. It is the
3,548-mile long route taken by Amundsen's ship *Gjøa*.

From Lunenburg to the Arctic Circle the distance is 1,950
miles, and from the Bering Strait to Vancouver, British Columbia,
another 2,500 miles. The entire journey from one part of civilization to another is about 8,000 miles long, and it *all* must be covered during the short northern summer. Get through the Arctic,
or . . . That was our task.

The crew that had signed on for the Northwest Passage was of
a rather particular makeup. From the day *Cigra* was launched in
Kraljevica, a lot happened in our club that was contrary to our
wishes and intentions. As the boat neared completion and the
voyage drew closer and closer, I began to get the feeling that some
members of the team were drawing back. This was incomprehen-
sible to me; after the feverish tempo of work and the efforts we
had made day and night, when the sweetest part of the work was
yet to come, stammering and unconvincing explanations began.

The first trial season in Greenland in 1994 had come off all
right, but when faced with the journey to the Arctic, our group
found itself in complete disarray. Problems at home, work, and all
kinds of excuses would probably never have surfaced if our destination had been Polynesia.

For a boat the size of *Cigra,* a five-man crew is too small.
Experience had shown me that, when there are seven or eight
capable people aboard, jobs are divided the most effectively and

everyone has time for everything—from maintaining the boat to having free time for writing, reading, and resting. But for the Northwest Passage, I did not have much choice. There were only four others, apart from myself, who were willing to set out on this uncertain voyage.

Three truckloads of provisions were stowed in space that became a "refrigerator"

Miro Muhek was an integral part of the project from the first day. He was a founder of our nautical club and had always been deeply involved in the plans. While the boat was still under construction, I had asked each member of the club to write down in which stage he would like to participate; Miro gave me not a move but a whole game. "I want to sail the whole expedition, from beginning to end," he told me. Serious and dependable, he stuck to his word, and his actions proved that he was the best possible man to have aboard—a person we could always rely on.[2]

Srecko Trajbar was a student. We included him in the voyage even though he hadn't taken part in the construction of the boat. He came highly recommended as a diver and competent climber; he was an intelligent and courageous lad.

Nenad Junek worked on marketing in the first part of the campaign. Since he had never sailed before, we had to teach him nautical skills. The only problem was that he could never manage to come to terms with seasickness, and his coffee and cigarette breaks lasted longer than usual some days.

Drago Ipsa literally flew into the crew at the last minute in

h ACIA

place of another person who defected at Vienna Airport two hours before his flight. In record time, Drago settled his family and business affairs so he could meet us in Lunenburg. We were all pleased that he managed to come, because we had had our "GHQ"—command central—in his cabin in Bakarac while the boat was being built in neighboring Kraljevica.

Previous attempts at getting through the Arctic have shown that the chances of mastering the entire passage in one season are almost zero, so we took some 1,600 kilos of food with us, the amount we estimated we would need to live on for 16 months if we were forced to winter over. The list was long and varied: 350 kg of flour, 80 tins of peas, 100 tins of carrots, 6 kg of yeast, 400 packets of soup, 50 tubes of various kinds of mustard, mayonnaise and horseradish; rice, lentils, and pasta; for cigarette smokers we limited their supply to one pack a day

Salami, cured ham shoulder and similar items were hung from the ceiling and we stowed 350 different kinds of provisions on shelves. To find our way around, we drew a special chart with plans of the numbered shelves and the arrangement of the food. In spite of this, the watch cook often had more difficulty finding the right provisions than actually preparing the dinner.

Our supplies also included plenty of fluids: 1,200 liters of water in two separate tanks, 18 bottles of rum and other alcoholic beverages, but not a drop of wine or beer. Before leaving Lunenburg, we bought one kit for making 20 liters of wine and a second for making 15 liters of beer. We invested a few tax-free dollars in the Canadian economy, because fruit juices, not alcohol, were needed to make the wine. To make the wine, we mixed three kinds of powder with grape concentrate, then waited 14 days for the mixture to ferment. We managed this only twice, since a precise, relatively high temperature is necessary and the barrel must be kept still—conditions almost impossible to achieve on this voyage. The main alchemist on board was Miro. Whenever I got angry with him, I would threaten to tell his father—who had his own cellar and a great reputation for wine-making—what his son was up to. We tried just once to make beer and gave up immediately; the swill we produced wasn't even worthy of being dumped into the head. It was a pity that we weren't able to lay in a better stock of liquids, but it was comforting to know that in the Arctic no one had ever died of thirst.

The wine-making jug was kept wrapped and fixed to the radiator, but conditions in the Labrador Sea did not lend themselves to success

Cigra and the five of us turned our stern on Greenland on July 23, 1995. Behind us we left Cape York, site of a memorial to the first man to reach the North Pole—the American, Robert E. Peary—and the highest latitude we were to reach, 76°02' N. At that moment we were only 838 miles from the Pole itself.

In the morning, as soon as I got up and went out on deck, my first thought was: "Just let me not see Greenland again." But the bum was still there; it is too high to disappear overnight. However, conditions in front of us were better. There

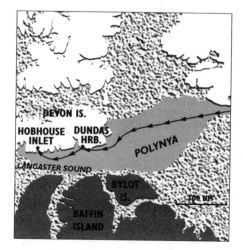

At last, after many long days, the engine had fallen silent

was *polynya*—a small area of open water without any ice. Somewhere to the west was the entrance into Lancaster Sound and Canada and, most important of all, we were sailing at full speed.

Far off in the north there are areas where the sea doesn't freeze, but these micro-climatic conditions are a rare exception, involving natural phenomena comprehensible only to scientists involved in the study of air and sea currents, geography and topography, physics and climatology.

The route the early whalers used to push through to the north, called the North-about-Passage, leads along the coast of Greenland, at distances less than three miles from land. It was along this route that we, too, managed to enjoy the pleasure of polynya and free sailing. If you have not undergone the torture of sailing through ice then you cannot understand what joy there is when you feel the movement of waves against the hull. What a relief, what a pleasure! Even sufferers of chronic seasickness enjoy it. The *polynya*, or North Water, as the whalers called the sea north of Baffin Bay, is a fairly large area. And so, sailing the 250 miles west from Greenland to Lancaster Sound in the Canadian Arctic was a "breeze" for us.

We revelled in the seascape, calling out to walruses that were stretched out on occasional ice floes. And, along the way, we were able to change the engine oil and make contact with two of the most important points in the Arctic—the town of Resolute and the icebreaker, *Henry Larsen*.

The pleasure of polynya

---

1. *Sailing Directions—Arctic Canada*, Vol 1, p. 1
2. Miro had the best command of English and often served as translator for the others.

chapter five

In the Wake of Amundsen

When you arrive in Canada, it's good practice, and obligatory anyway, to report to the authorities. Dundas Harbor, in Lancaster Sound, which Canadian *Sailing Directions* gives a cursory mention, is the only choice; the Royal Canadian Mounted Police (RCMP) building is located along its shore.

This celebrated police force guarded the Canadian frontier under very difficult conditions, keeping check on the movement of goldminers into Alaska, rustlers and smugglers to the south and spies to the north. The RCMP no longer exists in the region; the safety of the country is looked after in a more contemporary manner nowadays. But a memorial to these historical heroes remains—two or three huts, along with a few gravestones.

We reported to Customs by radio and had a good laugh. You go into a region where there isn't a living soul for thousands and thousands of miles; you don't know if there is any way out of the icy wastes at all or if you are going to stay alive, and then some naïve official calmly asks you whether you've still got the seal on the store in which you keep your 13 bottles of rum and meager supply of cigarettes.

But our circumstances were not in the least bit amusing. While planning the project, I had concluded that we could get through the Northwest Passage only if we arrived in the Arctic very early on. That is why we had ploughed into the ice of Melville Bay, in the heart of the Arctic, a month earlier than usual—much earlier than any other ship. Only one ship—an ice-

The former RCMP building in Dundas Harbour

breaker—had arrived before us that year; the season had not yet started.

Navigation of this area is possible only in August and September; Canadian icebreakers, headquartered in Halifax and St. John's, usually open up the path to the north in the first week of August. Until July, when we arrived, the sun hadn't yet begun its job, so conditions were still uncertain. We had succeeded thus far in our early push to the heart of the Arctic, but now we had to face the question of which way to continue.

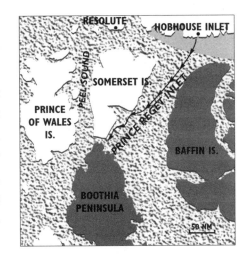

From radio conversations with people in Resolute and from details on the ice charts we received by fax, we had gained some important information:

A. Ahead of us, only 60 miles away, there was ice of a concentration of 9+[1] (a sheet two or three meters or 6–10 feet thick, cracked a bit here and there); 25 miles farther on it was a straight 10—another way of saying concrete—which not even the icebreakers will attempt. The bay of the town of Resolute was closed. In drift, close to Cornwallis Island, was the icebreaker *Henry Larsen,* engines off, waiting for conditions to change.

B. Someone had had a nasty mishap about 95 miles south of us. The 10-meter (32 foot) yacht *Roger Henry* was locked in ice at Tay Sound. The previous summer, Alvah Simon and his wife had attempted to sail to Thule, Greenland. In the *polynya* zone they were caught in a storm and sought shelter. After just a few hours,

Waiting for a change—for better or for worse

they were iced in and were forced to remain for 10 months. Alvah's wife was evacuated when it was learned that her father was dying in New Zealand. Alvah had spent part of the winter alone, shooting at polar bears with rubber bullets (an ecological statement made over the radio that we didn't take too seriously). He made a rather despondent call to us:

"The ice hasn't completely melted, but I hope the boat will be afloat in five or six days. Before that, I have to repair the rudder shaft which was twisted by the ice, and I've got a problem with the propeller."[2]

C. Possible routes onward, north of Somerset Island and through Peel Sound, were "paved" with number 10 ice, and the Canadians weren't even taking data for the really hopeless route that leads through Prince Regent Inlet.

Although we looked at all possible permutations based on the information in A, B and C, we could draw no sensible conclusion. I radioed Resolute for advice.

Bezal—whose High Arctic Explorers Inn is an overnight spot for pilots on rare flights to this "capital" of the Arctic—always has a short wave radio transmitter at hand like everyone else in the region so I asked him to get any information he could about the conditions of the ice.

He replied: "It's difficult, difficult. No one can advise you, no one wants to. In three or four weeks conditions will improve and then you can come to Resolute. Probably an icebreaker will push a path through one of these days. But now there's no chance at all. You've come too early. . . . I'll save a thousand or two liters of fuel for you and some food."

That's how it is in these icy waters. No one wants to shoulder the responsibility for others in these conditions, to give them advice or to make decisions for them. Everyone knows what the consequences of a wrong decision call might be in the Arctic.

Wait. They told us we had to wait; for days, perhaps weeks.

And in spite of everything, a wait sounded good; we needed a break. If only we could rest a bit and catch up on sleep at some anchorage. But, no! In the Arctic, nature doesn't let you relax. In Dundas Harbour, we had to shift position three times to prevent ice floes from constantly bashing into us and we were finally forced to sail out of the bay at three in the morning.

Miro and I had to maneuver for a long time before we were able to free the anchor. A great chunk of ice had pushed the chain to a depth of 78 meters (255 feet), and when we were raising the anchor, it got stuck in the underside of the ice, forcing us to put a several-ton load on the winch and electric motors. We escaped from the bay in the nick of time; just a few hours later, driven by some invisible force, great chunks of ice filled the entire bay, completely sealing the exit. We had come within a hair's breadth of ending up like Alvah's *Roger Henry.*

Entry into Hobhouse Inlet on Devon Island; the underwater bar which makes entry into the bay almost impossible is not shown on the charts

We radioed Canadian authorities that we were giving up the idea of sailing to Resolute, that we didn't need fuel, food or water, just lots of luck. I had decided to continue through the Arctic by a rather risky route, but one that, at the moment, was the only logical and possible way. Instead of following Amundsen's route through Lancaster Sound and Resolute to Barrow Strait and south in Peel Sound, I decided to head through Prince Regent Inlet, then through narrow Bellot Strait. Although he had chosen to pass through Barrow Strait and Peel Sound, our hero was Willy de Roos[3] whose book, *North-West Passage* was my bible while I was planning the expedition.

Arved Fuchs,[4] who had attempted the Northwest Passage just two seasons before us, had reasoned similarly. He tried to get through via Prince Regent Inlet and Bellot Strait but got jammed in pack ice in Prince Regent where he remained locked in for five days, almost losing his boat. When he finally reached the narrow strait, he couldn't get through so he turned back and followed Amundsen's route.

Of the other yachtsmen known to us, other than de Roos, only Clark Stede on *Asma* had opted for Bellot Strait; he got through in a single, fortunate, vigorous breath but then he got stuck on the opposite side. The Canadian Coast Guard had to send an icebreaker for him and, when they broke through to the *Asma*, in a risky maneuver they hoisted her on their deck and carried the boat and crew a hundred miles or so to open water.[5]

The Canadians in Ottawa and Resolute were surprised by our decision but made no comment. From that day on, they began faxing us ice charts for Prince Regent Inlet, and there was discreet sympathy and quiet rallying in the voice of the radio operator each time we called in our daily position.

The greatest quandary while sailing in an icy sea comes the moment you are confronted face to face with great masses of ice.

When it's land you're dealing with, the chart tells you very clearly which way to turn and how to avoid a given obstacle. But the ice knows no rules. It is an enormous, enigmatic wall, here today, somewhere else tomorrow, now under the bow, now forward of the bow.

How do you extricate yourself from such unpleasant, appalling situations? We had to determine by painstaking work and maneuvering whether the ice was thin enough to enter and break through. Thanks

The ice snaps and scrapes against the hull, *Cigra* rears and bucks, and the masts flex dangerously

to our experience in Melville Bay, we had discovered, little by little, what *Cigra* was capable of and what the limits of experimentation were.

If the ice was thicker than a meter and denser than 6/10, it was pointless to break through by force. So we would have to head left or right or leave the ice alone and simply stay where we were. Sometimes the best answer was to return to a safer position and select another route.

When this kind of problem presented itself, each member of the crew thought about things to himself, made calculations about risk and waited to see what the others would say. Not many

A moment of decision. In normal sailing conditions, the skipper can make a correct assessment in 95% of cases; here in the Arctic it is completely different

dared to think aloud, let alone propose something. They had too acute a feeling for the constant danger.

And so just one person—the captain—must make the decision, an irrevocable decision because, in the vast expanses of the Arctic, you know that in a week or two real winter, and still more ice, will be on its way.

During our conversation in Belgium, Willy de Roos had told

me, "Decisions about where to turn the boat always made me crazy. Yet in time, you begin to have a feel for this wretched ice. When you take into account everything around you—the current, the wind, the distance from land, the depth of the sea—you'll probably guess which way to head. But hesitating about whether left or right is better isn't very important. There's a passage on both sides, or there isn't one at all."

Sailing through Prince Regent Inlet toward Bellot Strait, we had to deal with about 35 miles of inevitable first-year or multi-year pack ice which has an average concentration of 5/10 to 8/10.

Here, the crew took up their usual positions: the lookout man in the barrel on the mast; the skipper on the roof of the wheelhouse; helmsman at the wheel; a fourth helping the helmsman with the engine commands; and the fifth zipping around the cockpit checking that the engine cooling water outlet was open, taking photographs, and handing out sandwiches.

The man in the crow's nest can last only 30 to 60 minutes. He's cold, the binoculars around his neck get in his way, and he has to work the buttons on the radio with gloves on. Every time the boat strikes the ice he thinks everything's up as the rigging sways

Sending out the inflatable helps assess conditions

perilously. He can see two or three miles beyond the boat and is the only one who has anything sensible to say. If other crew members disagree with his decisions, and later it turns out that he was wrong, it's usually too late. The only comfort then is to curse him.

The boat wanders around in the sea like a great clock, the bow being the hand at 12 o'clock and the stern at 6. From his height,

Our crow's nest, constructed of a 200-liter plastic barrel, was the most important item on board for the Arctic; better than radar and with a range of up to five miles, it was never subject to breakdowns

Multi-year pack ice in Prince Regent Inlet, risky for the hull because of its hardness

the lookout man gives radio messages more or less in this way:

"After this floe you've got a narrow passage at half-past nine; after that head straight for three o'clock. We've got about 30 minutes open water in that direction, and then a bit more to starboard. There's a narrow piece of pack ice we can break through. About 100 meters after that it's clear and we can get back on course."

Because GPS does not depend on the position and strength of the magnetic pole, navigation is easier; it calculates the course on the basis of real movement through the water, providing a new position every second or two

The helmsman listens and twirls the wheel furiously. The boat staggers, wanders like a drunk, but very quickly and adroitly gets around the ice barriers, going in circles and covering vast numbers of miles to no great forward advantage. The work of the helmsman is complicated and exhausting, especially if the lookout man hesitates in making a decision or gives directions that are not precise.

A narrow isthmus of about 100 meters separates Hazard Inlet from Depot Bay the area where, in 1987, ice forced David Scott Cowper to leave his converted lifeboat, *Mable E. Holland*, for the winter season

During the times when we're pushing through great sheets of ice, one man has the helm, another must be at the engine accelerator working it up or down.[6] The important job of the man in the cockpit is to check on the engine cooling system because ice will often block the cooling-water intake and then there's danger that the engine will overheat. This always happens at the moments of greatest strain, with the hull pushing or shoving aside tons and tons of ice mass. At times like this, lightning decisions and reactions are needed; the ship mustn't be allowed to stop in the ice, and the engine must have cooling water.

To prevent ice from freezing solid around the boat, the first and most important rule for going through ice runs is: "Don't, at any price, stop the boat. If you can't go forward, go back." Easy to say, but going into reverse is very hazardous because the first thing to hit the ice is the blade of the rudder, followed by the propeller. Accidents are almost inevitable and, in these conditions, they are often serious. What could you possibly do in mid-Arctic with your shaft buckled and your rudder blocked?

At the urging of ice experts in Lunenburg we had welded a mighty metal "beak" on the transom that was designed to sweep aside the ice when we were in reverse. For a joke, we called this invention "the big dick," but it really didn't deserve to be made fun of; it was a very smart idea and the most useful addition to *Cigra* since she left Kraljevica.

For a full 26 hours we pushed through the ice in Prince Regent Strait. We penetrated the ice field, the ice pounding the boat terrifically, its sharp edges scraping the sides and the transom. No one got more than 30 minutes sleep. Traces of *Cigra's* red bottom paint showed up on the floes. The fantastic pressure the plates and ribs had to endure was illustrated when a jet of ice was forced up through the narrow sink drain and shot out into the cabin.

At moments we sailed close to the shore where, under the warming influence of land and in shallows not marked on the chart, the ice is thinner and less concentrated. The next morning, a very strong sun, a cold wind and abnormal refraction of light[7] caused some of us to stagger and have hallucinations: the ice became open sea, the small floes gigantic bergs; narrow passages became fjords, and the boat's orienting clock went haywire several times. Fatigue and exhaustion created indescribable havoc. In the end, it was only accidentally, thanks to a strong current, that we noticed a tricky sandbar. We headed around it and entered a large bay in which there was not too much ice. Salvation! When we came into the bay, we discovered that it had an ominous name—Hazard Inlet. Irony or mistake? I wondered. I hit the wall and turned in.

---

1. 90% ice

2. See *North to the Night—A Year in the Arctic Ice* by Alvah Simon, McGraw Hill International Marine Division

3. Willy de Roos mastered the Northwest Passage, from east to west in his yacht *Williwaw* in 1977. His exploit was unique in many ways. Having gone through the same torture as he did, we can give credible confirmation to his accomplishment. Until Gjøa Haven, de Roos had one other crewman aboard. Then, the way things often go, his crewman left and de Roos had to go solo through inconceivable efforts to reach Vancouver in late autumn of the same year. He was greeted as a hero when he arrived.

4. Arved Fuchs, trained in the navy, has taken part in 14 expeditions. He reached both the South and the North poles on foot, in the same calendar year; went to Cape Horn in a kayak; and has crossed the Atlantic several times. When, for reasons beyond his control, he did not manage to circumnavigate the North Pole along the Norway-Northeast Passage-Labrador Sea route, he decided on the Northwest Passage, completing it in a single season on *Dagmar Aaen*. The Canadians hold it against him that he did not ask permission.

5. Clark Stede, journalist, photographer and sailor with 60,000 miles of experience, set out with an Australian, Michelle Poncini, planning to spend a winter in the Northwest Passage for which they had prepared. However, things got out of control and, off Hepburn Point, pack ice pushed them on shore.

6. Because the helmsman must give his complete attention to the wheel, someone else must work the throttle.

7. This Arctic glare, known as "ice blink," had a detrimental effect on the crew.

chapter six

The Inuit in Gjøa Haven

We spent nine unforgettable days in the vicinity of Hazard Inlet on Somerset Island where nothing was ordinary or easy. We had entered a bay we could no longer sail out of; the wind had shoved an ice field about 60 miles wide onto the island and shut off the entrance and any chance of our making it through to the east entrance of Bellot Strait, five miles away.

It is hard to imagine, but try conjuring up a frozen surface the size of the Adriatic. For example, you've entered Stupica Bay on the island of Zirje, then a southerly brings ice, blocking the exit, and there's no turning back. You spend your days of captivity walking on shore, guarding every step you take with a powerful shotgun, in futile expeditions hunting for musk ox to vary your menu, and sleeping in the former Hudson's Bay hut called Fort Ross[1] which you have to sprinkle with formaldehyde before going to bed to keep away the polar bears. What's more, the Ice Patrol plane flies overhead with a message:

"There's an ice field of concentration 9+ stretching as far as the opposite coast. The situation is the same as it was when we were here 10 days ago. In the strait you're intending to go

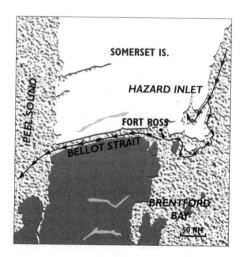

51

With its pup near a breathing hole, the seal (Pagophilus groenlandicus) is an easy prey for the polar bear

through, the concentration of ice is 10 in places, and almost 60 percent of the rest of the area is covered in 9+ ice. The sea behind you is 9+ too. How on earth did you get through? . . . Good luck!"

Then they hurriedly fly away, certain that you have a carbine on board with a good telescopic sight.

In this case, a northeasterly is your only salvation. Not just *any* northeasterly, but one with a force of at least 25 to 30 knots lasting at least three days, the time it will take for this whole layer—about 60 miles wide—to move 150 meters and open a navigable route along the edge of the island.

These external difficulties had their effect on the crew. Feeling so close to danger, they lost their good humor. However, before we left Hazard Inlet, we spent two days celebrating after we heard a short wave broadcast that Knin, a town 150 miles from Zagreb, had been liberated by the Croatian military. Then, luck was with us; a westerly wind of the right strength and intensity began to shift the ice, very slowly.

We tried to get out of the trap, but we didn't succeed at first.

An ice field 60 miles wide in Hazard Inlet; except in the shallows close to shore where depths are just a meter, there is no way through the ice unless some great force pushes it away

We returned to the anchorage and, just to make it more "amusing," ran aground in a place where the chart shows depths of 16 meters. The mood of the crew quickly plummeted to zero.

Salvation came an hour after midnight: musk-ox sighted on the banks of the inlet released our negative charges in a different direction. Afterward, the crew were all present and accounted for, and

I spent three nights in the attic here in Fort Ross; with a bit of elevation, it was the only way I could check the changes in the state of the ice every three to four hours

The former Hudson's Bay trading post at Fort Ross has a few pots and pans, some fuel and instructions for filing a report in case you have to shoot a polar bear in self-defense

so were the musk-ox—it is not easy to be a hunter! The following day, the ice sheet had shifted some 70 meters, enabling us to get through the next five miles to Depot Bay.

The watches had been carefully observing the rhythm of high and low tides for four days; the direction and speed of the current in the strait depended on it. And I myself was keeping an eye on the ice conditions in Bellot Strait. The strait which is 18 miles long and less than a mile wide deserves to be called a *narrows*; the current which changes here four times a day is a bit stronger at the eastern entrance, sometimes attaining a velocity of eight knots. Where the strait curves, ice builds up, blocking the passage.

An opportunity suddenly cropped up when, at four in the morning, I noticed a change in the center of the strait. At 0800 hours I sent a scout into the strait in our inflatable and at 1130 his order came over the radio: "Move!"

We mastered the 18-mile-long strait in two hours and fifteen minutes. Ice floes rushed through with us and, with the current flowing at 8 knots, they turned into deadly torpedoes. We received a few fierce thumps, the ice scraping *Cigra*'s sides, but we managed to get through on the western side of the strait.

Miro, who was always up to the job, calmly said: "Who says 13 is an unlucky number?" And so it was that, on August 13, 1995, we sailed into the West Arctic, as this area is officially called.

Srecko climbed down from the crow's nest and I took out the last two bottles of champagne, explaining my generosity to an astounded crew: "One is for this unlucky Bellot; the second is because we're at the point of no return. Cheers!" It had taken us exactly nine days and four hours to make the 21 miles from Hazard Inlet to Depot Bay and Fort Ross, and then through Bellot Strait.

Raold Amundsen, one of the most courageous explorers of the Twentieth Century

In the first year of his Arctic voyage in 1903, Amundsen got as far as a little bay on King William Island, neither very deep nor very large, but well protected from winds and waves and, in his opinion, an ideal spot for wintering over. (And Amundsen already had a lot of experience since he spent one winter a captive of the ice in the ship *Belgica* in 1897.)

In the middle of September of that year, the snow began to fall. His seven-man crew unloaded freight from *Gjøa* and set up a small camp on the coast, on the very eve of the autumnal equinox—the beginning of the long arctic night. Not long afterward, five or six Inuits appeared,

Gjøa Haven

and little by little they began to trust each other. They asked Amundsen if they could settle there, and then, out of the snow-storm loomed a whole tribe, 200 people who set up camp close to the ship. Thus Amundsen and his crew became the first Europeans to make genuine contact with the Inuit. In the end, they spent 19 months together.

The bold and capable Norwegian explorers had fore-seen everything ex-

There are fewer and fewer classic canoes; most of the boat are aluminum or fiberglass like this one

cept an exceptionally cold summer the following year. When the ice in Gjøa Bay, named after their ship, failed to melt during the summer months of 1904, the Inuit and Norwegians went hunting and fishing together. They

Houses in Gjøa Haven are raised above ground because of the permafrost

gave him whole-hearted support in his meteorological and magnetic measurements, and when *Gjøa* finally sailed away, the Inuit remained in the bay, and they are still there.

In Greenland, they had warned us that when we spoke to them we should use the word Inuit, which means *the people*—the word Eskimo has a pejorative meaning for them, being translated from the Cree language as people who eat raw flesh.[2]

Now, after 33 days of sailing, we saw living people again—the Inuit in Gjøa. There is order among these Canadian Inuit. They respect the law, they are well organized and, considering the harsh arctic conditions, they live well. They drive small 4WD bikes and wear helmets. In summer the children go naked, the men hunt for fish, seals, whales, and they obtain everything they need from nature.

Arctic char, which tastes very much like salmon, is plentiful and easy to catch from shore

The Canadian government has provided

decent, kit houses for them and, at considerable trouble and ex-
pense, supplies them with heating oil.[3]

In their kitchen, although they have a table, they spread card-
board over the floor and eat their meal sitting on the floor. Their
diet usually consists of raw or dried, unsalted, fish and meat.
Since average temperatures in winter are about -30°C (-22°F),
their houses are well-insulated; their water tank is usually located
inside the house with a septic tank below it, both of which have
their own heaters. When temperatures drop below -70°C (-94°F),
they begin to worry.

We visited the Amundsen Hotel and found that they serve
only coffee and soft drinks. At the Amundsen Market, prices—as
high as those in Greenland—are 60 percent higher than the rest
of Canada.

We telephoned our families back home. Then, unlike
Amundsen, who spent 22 months in Gjøa, we stayed just 22
hours. This was a nice place, but there was no sense in going
"overboard."

In the waters west of Gjøa we came upon the small yacht *Dove
III* which was sailing in the opposite direction—west to east—
with three bearded musketeers from Vancouver Island. When we
tied them alongside *Cigra*, surprise followed surprise. The only
identification they had with them was an ordinary business card
on which was printed:

Dove III–Arctic Expedition
Captain: Winston Bushnell
First Mate: George Hone, Naturalist
Artist: Len Sherman

We looked over the 8-meter-long steel sailboat which, as the
captain and owner said, was built "especially for the Northwest
Passage." In the center of our salon, where we had a dining table,
they had a toilet without a cover. They heated by ordinary wood

stove and we could-
n't see wood any-
where on board.
Their navigation
desk was no bigger
than a child's picture
book; they had no
short-wave radio
station, and canned
food was stowed all
over their bunks.

They took a look
around our craft and
their voices gave
them away at once.
Then they grew
silent; it was obvious
they found our ves-
sel luxurious com-
pared to theirs, and
it was fortunate that
our central heating
wasn't working at
the time, because if
they had touched a

The brave crew of *Dove III*

radiator, it would have been the last straw for them.

We parted soon, giving them a brief description of what was in store for them and explaining our route through the Arctic. They warned us of what lay ahead, and Bushnell told me: "You've got about 500 miles of open water to the west, but watch yourselves in Alaska; it's really hairy there. But wait . . . where do I know you from? Off the Cape of Good Hope I capsized in a 10-meter yacht, and I spent six months repairing it in Capetown.

Did we maybe meet there?"

During the whole conversation, I was feverishly wondering what we could do for these men, give them a bit of equipment, anything that might be useful; but it was only after we parted that I realized we could have given them two cans of fuel. For them it would have been a big reward.[4]

The meeting had a good effect on our crew; for the first time on the voyage, one of my Arctic heroes stopped taking Valium for at least 10 days.

---

1. The former Hudson's Bay trading post at Fort Ross has a few pots and pans, some fuel, and instructions for filling out a report in case you have to shoot a polar bear in self-defense.

2. We had said goodbye to the Greenland Eskimos—the word suits them better, after all. In the village of Kraulshaven, 74° N, they live very primitively, more than 40% with tuberculosis. This is not surprising when they throw their trash right in front of their houses and are surrounded by swarms of disgusting flies.

3. The oil, electricity, water and sewage cost $820 (Canadian) per household per month.

4. *Arctic Odyssey* (Fine Edge) by artist Len Sherman is an account of *Dove III*'s voyage.

chapter seven

Dangerous Pack Ice

The Arctic is a moving ice-island. That is why there is no point in building a base on it; everything would soon shift from its coordinates. And unlike Antarctica, its foundations could well melt away some day.

But there is more than ice in the Arctic—there are also islands, so low that for decades they couldn't be distinguished from the ice. This created problems for mapmakers and people who wanted to find a sea route. People who come to the Arctic in boats, rather than sleds, face another problem—shallow water.

Treacherous ice in the Beaufort Sea

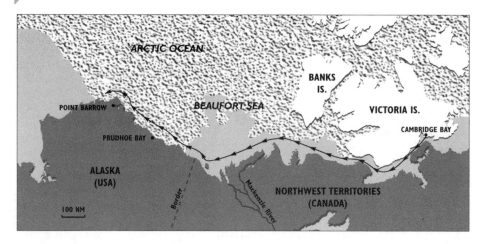

The unwritten law of the region does not recommend sailing through these waters in a vessel with a draft of over 1.5 meters (5 feet). Our calculated draft of 1.85 meters became 2.10 meters (about 6–7 feet) due to the weight of the cargo—a big handicap.

For this reason, the sight of the high Alaskan mountains and entry into the Beaufort Sea was a pleasant change, as well as a relief. But this was not the end of a weary tale; we were still far from being able to celebrate completing the Northwest Passage in one season. I was familiar with all the attempts to get through the Arctic and I knew there was one more barrier in front of us, one that is frequently insurmountable—*multi-year* pack ice from the

Hurrah! the mountains of Alaska at last

Arctic Ocean that rises a meter or two above the surface of the sea. It is dense, tough and dangerous, with crystals that have changed their chemical structure over the years making the ice as hard as steel.

One particular problem about sailing in the Beaufort Sea is that between Alaska and the North Pole there are no islands, and the entire mass of ice that stretches all the way to Siberia moves under the influence of the winds, the currents and the Coriolis forces.[1]

In Cambridge Bay, the commander of the tug that brought the barges loaded with annual supplies, had lent us 29 charts of Alaska to photocopy. He also drew in his navigation routes and gave me this advice: "Stick to the coast the whole time. Only in the shallows is there open water. The ice in this region has a draft of six or seven meters, and the only possible way through is in the narrow coastal zone between the sandy beaches and ice floes that have grounded. Don't even dream of setting out into the open sea, farther from the coast. Don't kid yourselves about the open sea. If the ice captures you there . . . bye-bye. You wouldn't be the first boat who was never heard of again."

The American and Canadian *Pilots* give the same advice. The American book adds:

> *Multi-year pack ice is good and bad. On the one hand it has depth and it can be gone round in shallows, on the other hand it is a serious threat even to icebreakers. It is never recommendable to get away from the coast.*
>
> *Anyone who remains in the area of the Beaufort Sea after September is exposing himself to great danger. Point Barrow has to be rounded before the end of the month, anything else being imprudent and foolish . . .*

As we sailed across the demarcation line and entered American waters, we found ourselves in this pack ice. So far, it had been bearable because the Mackenzie River, with the second largest drainage basin in the world after the Amazon, has enormous power in the summer, nudging ice away from the coast. But the

After 66 days and 3958 miles, we crossed the demarcation line; the Northwest passage had been mastered!

remaining 400 miles to Point Barrow were a real nightmare. Autumn was fast approaching, giving us less and less time. Snow was already fluttering across the deck, the rigging was frozen, and the crew were becoming increasingly exhausted.

During my watch in the early morning of September 1, as *Cigra* was close to Herschel Island, I spotted a ship on the horizon. In the Arctic, this is so sensational that I almost veered from our course to pass closer to it. The Canadian Coast Guard are well aware of who is navigating in their waters, and three or four ships wandering around in the Arctic can easily be identified despite the fact that the area covers hundreds of thousands of square kilometers. They were on the air at once:

"Yacht *Croatian Tern*, the icebreaker *Louis St. Laureant* is calling you." This really perked us up because the biggest Canadian icebreaker was quite familiar to us; we had visited it a year earlier in the harbour of Halifax,

August in the Arctic Ocean

just after its return from the
North Pole.

The commander was satis-
fied when he saw that we were
in good condition, and he was
pleased when he heard that we
knew what his bridge and gym
looked like, as well as the helicopter hangar.

A half-hour after our first
contact, their helicopter flew
over us and went scouting. A
short time later they radioed us about the latest ice conditions
and sent us a weatherfax. Their information suggested that it
would be better, faster and easier to sail farther offshore for the
next 400 miles; not in the shallows, but at a distance of some 35
to 40 miles in ice that the ice chart showed as:

Zone A: concentration 1 to 4. Zone B: concentration 5 to 9+.

Following Arctic protocol, we received no answer from the ice
observer to our question about whether it might be dangerous to
move away from shore. He said only: "That's the situation. It's
not bad, although Zone B is obviously impassable for you. But
you never know. Things could change quickly."

The route they suggested went through Zone B for 115 miles
—a mere fleabite.

From there to Point Barrow, our everyday life was quite interesting. The ship's compass stopped turning madly and, after two
months of voyaging through the Arctic, it began to give courses
with an error of *less than* 180°! Then we began to experience night
again: three or four hours of darkness in which traversing the ice
field became a totally absorbing discipline.

Every piece of Beaufort pack ice was a minefield that made the
Greenland growlers look like children's toys. One night we

Polar bear in the distance (indicated in the circles)

managed to slip through somehow; then we spent the next two nights floating in the ice at minimum rpms, just maintaining steerage; the fourth night we anchored 15 miles from the coast.

As a farewell to these horrors, our last day in the ice brought a nice surprise. Srecko, who was searching for a way out of a difficult situation, yelled down from the crow's nest:

"Polar bears at nine o'clock! Mother and cub."

The helmsman turned immediately. We came to a sudden, rough stop and discovered that it wasn't a mother and her cub but two adults; visible against the ice because their fur was yellowish.

Bushnell had warned me not to stop at Prudhoe Bay. "Just imagine," he told us, "We got into the richest oil field in Alaska and they drove us off like dogs. They didn't even give us a drop of fuel." And so it happened that we never did see the Alaskan coast. Sightseeing in Prudhoe Bay—the biggest oilfield in Alaska—had to be postponed for another time. We didn't even see any oil rigs, and the only thing I remember is the tip of the mast of a Japanese yacht anchored in Barrow whose skipper—we had learned—lives most of the time on the ice, studying permafrost. There was apparently a Croat plumber living in the village, too, but we decided to postpone meeting him until our next visit—perhaps when we want to install a hot water heater into *Cigra*.

We said a disdainful farewell to the last piece of ice some 20 hours after rounding Point Barrow, the northernmost point of the USA[2] and, with an excellent wind, we were able to sail rapidly through the Chukchi Sea, then turn and make our southward run. On September 8, we crossed the Arctic Circle and, 9 hours later that same day, sped through the Bering Strait. Rain and bad weather prevented us from sighting Siberia, just 18 miles away, except on the radar screen. Here behind us, the door to the North-west Passage shut.

We had logged a total of 3,958 miles in 66 days, 12 hours. And, as far as we knew, *Cigra* was the 57th boat, including ice-breakers, ever to traverse the passage; the fifth yacht to have done it in one season—12 days faster than the previous record. There was reason, then, to celebrate, so we altered our planned route and tied up in the village of Nome, famous for its

Nome, the once and present "city of gold"

Dutch Harbor in the Aleutians, one of the richest fishing ports in the world

goldminers and everything that goes with such an adventurous business.

Assuming that, in this "metropolis of Northwest Alaska"—as the U.S. *Coast Pilot* calls it—there would be no prohibition, we looked forward to a well-deserved celebration. We suspected we'd be able to find a pub—and intuition is an important trait of every seafarer.

---

1. Spinning of the earth.

2. The most northerly point of the North American continent lies at the tip of Boothia Peninsula, in Bellot Strait.

chapter eight

Paradise for Orcas

An easterly wind off the coast brought us the sweet smell of land, the sound of birds twittering, and the knowledge that we were approaching tamer regions. We could smell the heavy but glorious scent of pines.

Against this, the odor of goulash spread from the galley into the cockpit; it was goulash of the worst kind from a tin that not even the military wants to use. I can't name it—it was neither of Irish nor Canadian origin, but a "gift" from back home.

The cook of the day had created this wild combination of odors at the very moment we were approaching the coast of British Columbia and its marvelous forests. With polite excuses, we declined supper and concentrated on the voyage through the narrow channels where, in addition to the usual problems of navigating at night, we had to avoid giant logs, weighing hundreds of kilos, that lie half-submerged under the surface. Saturated with water, these are growlers of another kind!

On a boat with a five-man crew, the rhythm is such that there is a different cook on watch every day. His duties in the galley don't free him from

The dense forests of British Columbia are an untouched haven for deer

his other daily tasks, or from his obligatory five hours at the helm. The duty cook has to prepare tea and coffee early in the morning, breakfast at 0900, a snack at about 1300 and a fairly large dinner before twilight which, of course, is impossible in the Arctic in summer. And apart from cooking, he has the washing-up to do—lots of fun, since it must be done in cold sea water. The temperature of the sea, in which the detergent has to foam and remove the grease, ranges from 26°C (78°F) in the tropics to -1.3°C (34°F) close to the poles. And the average sea temperature during the whole of our journey was less than 10°C (50°F).

At a later hour, when the crew are warming their toes in their sleeping bags, the cook—spattered with flour and grease, hands red from cold water, and mad because he hasn't had enough praise—will shout out:

"That's it! Galley's closed. Damn you, wasn't even the fruit salad any good?"

After this cry, everything becomes the worry of tomorrow's condemned man whose day starts with washing the cups and glasses that have accumulated during the night. Before breakfast he has to check on the state of the bread, because it is on the bread and on the cook that the beginning of our day depends.

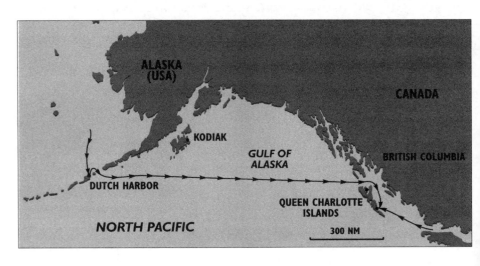

The magical channels of British Columbia in autumn rain

Here's a lightning sketch of our cooking skills (I won't identify the individuals by name!):

Person 1 has a good hand and a fair amount of experience. Back in Greenland he asked me to buy additional gear for peeling potatoes, because for him no meal was any good if it didn't include potatoes. He comes from a part of Croatia where cautious and rational handling of food is in the blood, a quality which the skipper values more than the crew who care only about filling their stomachs. He is keenest on making coffee several times a day, even when he's not on watch. His main specialty is potato gnocchi. On Somerset Island, while we were waiting for Bellot Strait to de-ice and the tide to take the boat off the beach, our rifle just happened to go off. Young musk-ox meat and potato gnocchi—there's nothing better!

Person 2 cooks in silence, without a lot of talk. He most likes prosciutto and prepares it every time he is on duty. He also likes cake, and honey cakes and pepper biscuits occasionally figure on his menu. I allowed him to serve breakfast at 1200, because he

A 50-knot northwesterly in the Gulf of Alaska had given us quite a shake-up

had to stand watch until 0500 and needed to catch a bit of sleep before cooking.

Person 3 cooks eggs in variety of ways, but his specialty i pizza. He is the only one who knows how to prepare game and bread dumplings. He is usually about an hour late putting food on the table, but it's worth being patient.

Person 4 has a bigger appetite than usual, and that is his *onl* thing in common with the kitchen. If only we could have fasted every fifth day when it was his turn in the galley! He feeds us in various ways with canned foods, usually served cold. The precis combination of rusty tins and half-moldy rusk depends on hi mood. He washes dishes at such speed that they may be clean by let's say, breakfast the next morning.

Person 5 doesn't mind the galley too much and thinks of the tasks required as a necessary routine that has to be performed Since life on board is full of abnormal situations, little sleep, a lo of fatigue and other rapidly changing events, he tries to cook a

well as he can, given the conditions. He doesn't like making
coffee or soup, but he is good at
marinades. Whenever possible
he swaps washing dishes for
cooking with some other crew
member.

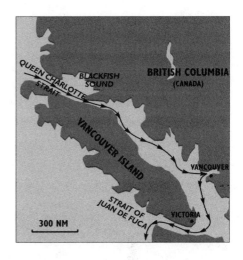

We never economized on
food, either quantity or quality,
and always had plenty to eat.

In the calm channels of B. C.,
Cigra finally settled down. The
wilds of the ocean were now replaced by beautiful islands and
bays where we could see the trees rising right from the water,
smell the conifers, hear the sound of birds, and spot deer and bear
quietly moving through the bush. Once again, after five months,
we felt that life existed. It was a welcome change because the Gulf
of Alaska had given us quite a shaking-up. As we were crossing
the 1,200-mile-wide gulf, the remains of autumn typhoons above
Japan waltzed over the north Pacific, hitting us at a speed of eight,
10 or even 12 on the Beaufort scale; one night we measured a
wind of 74 knots. We lost the rail on the stern and sailed our 50-
ton boat at a speed of five or six knots with only a 10^2-meter
storm jib.

Our speed would have been greater still if we hadn't been tow-
ing 200 meters (650 ft.) of line off the stern for stability. We nearly lost both inflatable dinghies when giant waves poured over the
davits and began tearing at the blocks and lines. The genoa furl-
ing gear blew into 1,000 pieces, and later, in a Force 10 gale, the
crew somehow managed to lower the 90^2-meter genoa without
falling overboard. We weren't able to estimate the height of the
waves because the storm occurred during the night.

Drago was a great hand at the wheel in these moments, but

Orcas

poor Zeljko, who had come aboard at Dutch Harbor in the Aleutians, hit the third and final stage of his sea sickness.

For anyone who hasn't experienced it, this underhand torturer of the yachtsman works slowly but persistently:

Stage I: You feel so bad you *think* you're going to die.

Stage II: You feel so bad you are *sure* you're going to die.

Stage III: You feel so bad you *want* to die.

As far back as Dutch Harbor, I had altered our original plan of sailing down the Pacific and entering Juan de Fuca Strait, near the southernmost point of Vancouver Island, to reach Vancouver. It had become clear that we were all too tired to continue in outside waters. So, from there, I had ordered 32 charts that would enable us to enter the channels of British Columbia. The charts were sent by air from Seattle in just two days. With the help of these charts we entered Queen Charlotte Strait, passing through Blackfish Sound and Johnstone Strait at the north end of Vancouver Island.

If you know that orca is the Indian name for the black-fish, and that Johnstone Strait is one of the richest areas in Canada for salmon, then there must be killer whales around. Unfairly called killers, these mammals are said to be the most intelligent crea-

The orca's trademark is its vertical dorsal fin and white belly

tures in the sea; they like eating well and in abundance, and their favorite food is the salmon.[1]

We came across these orcas off Robson Bight where the Tsitika River drains into Johnstone Strait. Two adult whales and three or

Sixteen fishing boats came out to welcome us in Vancouver

four calves entertained us for over two hours. The bolder ones dove under the hull several times and when the youngsters had convinced themselves that *Cigra* was not their mummy, they swam elegantly off.

Who's on galley watch today?

Orcas live in families called pods, and they always swim together. The females are fertile for about 20 years, and an adult pair will have two or three young. Their average life span is 60 to 70 years, and granddad and grandma enjoy playing with their grandchildren.

We continued down through Johnstone Strait, and crossed the Strait of Georgia where 16 fishing boats from Vancouver's Croatian colony came out to meet us and escorted us to a place of honor in front of Vancouver's Maritime Museum. It was a welcome and fitting end to the first season of our expedition.

---

1. In Antarctica, penguin is a delicacy for them. With a flip of their powerful tail, they simply overturn an ice floe on which these gentlemen in their tuxes are sunning themselves.

chapter nine

North America to Pitcairn

Cigra spent the winter of 1995-96 on the Fraser River in Vancouver in a shipyard similar to the one in Lunenburg on the Atlantic side of Canada. Surrounded by saw mills, barges full of sawdust and logs floating down-river, and in rain and dampness, we kept the boat heated with some strong light bulbs, exterminated the algae in the tanks, and waited for spring.

When spring arrived, the owner of the shipyard, Tomislav Serka—one of our countrymen—raised *Cigra* on the slipway for several days, and put his welders and turners to work. His enterprising Croatian workers cut off the bow reinforcement and the protection around the propeller and installed new decking on the

Cigra wintered in Vancouver at the TOM-MAC marina and shipyard

bowsprit. Tomislav lent us his tools and, when I asked for the bill, he waved his hands, indicating no money was due.

"Good luck, lads" he told us. "Glad to have been able to help you. See you at home, on Brac Island.[1]"

During our voyage to San Francisco, we were visited by four members of the U.S. Coast Guard for half an hour. They happened to choose a time when the wind was

The U.S. Coast Guard checking up on *Cigra*

blowing 35 knots, the waves were high, and *Cigra* was sailing at seven or eight knots. They hurried over from their Coast Guard cutter in an inflatable with a crew of eight.

While four of them (unarmed according to regulations) inspected the boat, our documents and weapons, four others remained in the inflatable as back-up. They kept in touch with each other by radio, and they also had a direct link with the cutter standing off a few miles away. It was obvious that the gentlemen in the inflatable each had some bulky items concealed under their thick waterproof suits.

We had a pleasant, if short, stay in San Francisco where our hosts were our own countrymen and the Croatian Catholic Mission. While we were there, U.S. Customs realized, as they had in Nome a year earlier, that *Cigra* was not a merchant ship and that there was no need to charge us $820 to tie up in every port.

After endless talks, our troubles ended with a sticker that cost us $25 for a whole year. The officials gave us a warning that I had been familiar with for years: It is forbidden to sail into ports and bays or to dock where U.S. Customs does not have an office.

From San Francisco, we headed south to San Pedro, a suburb of Los Angeles, where we gave a presentation about our expedition; in San Diego, we acquired a bit of equipment, some charts and repair parts. We continued south to Mexico where we "lost" our weapons. Some soldiers in Turtle Bay climbed aboard and confiscated both our rifles.

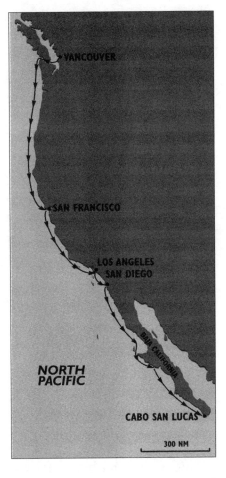

"It's just temporary," said a whiskered commander of the garrison. "You will get them back again in Cabo San Lucas when you leave Mexican territorial waters." His eyes narrowed as if even he didn't believe his own words.[2]

Miro tried to protest, but I was actually relieved. Since there would be no polar bears in Antarctica, it was best to get rid of the guns. For self-defense we had a 9-meter genoa pole, two rusty machetes, and two spray cans of mace for hand-to-hand combat. Weapons were not for us; they can only get you into hot water.

Once, in Palermo, just owning the rifles had caused me a lot of trouble and I was forced to spend two unplanned nights in an institution called Urdiccone—the best guarded jailhouse in Italy. This

We set a lively pace with our genaker, a cross between a Genoa and a spinnaker

facility hosts some 2,300 individuals who are serious criminals.

When the misunderstanding was cleared up, my reputation in certain circles in Palermo suddenly shot up. We were fed *gratis* for several days and the port police, who had instigated the whole thing, tried to make it up to us by preparing some meals on the *Cigra*, by giving little gifts to Tanja, and engaging in ham radio conversations while we were sailing toward Gibraltar.

We sailed halfway across the Pacific Ocean in 22 days—a stretch of 2,980 miles from Cabo San Lucas, at the very tip of Baja California, to the island of Nuku Hiva in the Marquesas. The Marquesas, which lie about 700 miles northeast of Tahiti, are an attractive archipelago composed of 12 small

The dolphins were friendlier than the officials

but high volcanic islands.

Our route took a rather unusual curve because, as usual, the weather did not follow either the forecasts, the statistics, or the 100-year averages shown on the pilot charts.

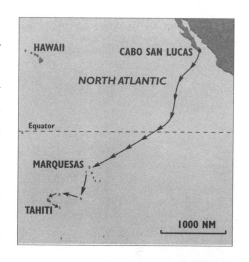

We set a lively pace at the beginning, faster than usual, for hurricane Alma was boiling up behind our stern, generating winds of 105 knots. Near the equator we were slowed by the doldrums, but after that we averaged 150 to 160 miles a day in the trade winds, landing precisely in the same bay where Herman Melville deserted the whaling ship and began acquiring the experiences he would later draw upon for his novel *Typee*.

A baptismal for the first-timers crossing the Equator

With the help of the southeast trades, we dropped down to the southernmost Polynesian islands and, with south winds abeam, turned to the east. From a distance of 9.2 miles,

The GPS shows the magical line; most sailors agree that it is best to cross between 125° and 130° of longitude where the doldrums are narrowest

we saw the island of Fangataufa which, together with neighboring Mururoom, was the center of the French nuclear tests.

Arriving on the island of Mangareva, we said farewell to an earthly paradise, for Polynesia's Austral islands are not exactly the tropics. "Stanislaw," the island's chief of police, was an exiled Pole who kindly allowed us to wash our dirty laundry in the police station and fill up with water from his filters. He had received a fax from Papeete giving us special per-
mission from the
police and the
Quai d'Orsai to
visit the "forbid-
den test zone."

One night,
our mischievous
students on *Cigra*
hid 60 kilograms
of bananas on the

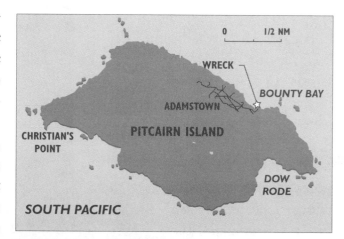

Horseracing is a common sight in Tiaohae Bay on Nuku Hiva

Bounty Bay is open, bare and unprotected—not at all pleasant

bow under the inflatable. Of course, we did not admit this to the Pole. He was more interested in who on the island used *paco loco* (something like marijuana, but much better and 10 times stronger, they say), and who broke the law by selling liquor on Sunday. He also wanted to return to France as soon as possible.

On Pitcairn Island, we met the descendants of the *Bounty* mutineers. They are essentially prisoners who cannot escape; the island is completely isolated from the rest of the world and the restless ocean makes it hard to get to them or for them to leave.

We anchored in Bounty Bay at a depth of 16 meters (52 feet); the bay is an open roadstead, unprotected, with a hard rocky bottom that requires a good deal of acrobatic skill and a great amount of courage for a successful disembarkation. The anchorage has been the site of frequent shipwrecks caused by anchors that failed to hold. The *H.M.S. Bounty* itself was burned and scuttled here in 1790. On average, 20 yachts a year sail past Pitcairn and only four or five of them attempt to land their tender an equipment. They must be adventurous, lucky, and have a crew crazy enough to risk their own lives as they hurtle up a diagona ramp between two waves.

Two miles long and a mile wide, Pitcairn today is home to 4 people, some of whom are genuine descendants of Fletche Christian and his followers. (A freckled-faced lady told us proud ly, "I am one of them.") The island is off all shipping route: 4,100 miles from Panama, 3,300 from New Zealand and 1,35 from Tahiti.

Back in 1789, Christian, the first officer of the ship *Bount* who had a dose of aristocratic blood and a good upbringing, seize control of the ship that had been sent by the British Admiralty t Polynesia for bread fruit plants. The main cause of the mutiny wa dissention in the crew which developed when they were unable t master the infamous Cape Horn. The energetic, capable captair William Bligh, tried for days to round the Horn, wearing out th crew, ruining the ship and the sails, and depleting the food suppl but he could not conquer the last 20 miles.

When they arrived in Polynesia by another route, the muti neers put Bligh in an open boat with the men who were loyal t him. Bligh went one way; Fletcher Christian, in the *Bounty*, wer another, finally reaching this isolated island in the middle of th Pacific. Nine mutineers in all landed on the island, along with si Tahitian men, twelve Tahitian women, and one little girl. The set fire to the ship, hoping that the search the English would cer tainly mount would not be successful.

In the 25 hours we spent anchored in Bounty Bay, we got t know half the population and the four radio ham operators wh are the islanders' only link to the rest of the world. The teache who had come from New Zealand, sees to the education of fiv children. Her husband occupies himself with fishing and lookin

Tanja and our baby, Ana, joined us in Tahiti where, Ana forsook fruit juices for coconut milk

after the school and a little museum. To be courteous, we bought a few souvenirs carved out of wood which they gather from near-by Henderson Island, a few postage stamps—their main source of revenue—and some publications. The islanders gave us some eggs and a lot of vegetables which grow in abundance; they also sold us some Chilean wine.

In the midst of this unreal location, set in the vastness of the Pacific, everything surprised us. A small diesel generator provides electricity for Pitcairn four hours a day; every house has a television set (good only for videos since there is no reception), and a large refrigerator. The houses are linked by an intercom system and by radio. Water from a spring is piped around the island through PVC piping suspended from the lamp posts. The islanders use small 4-wheel Honda bikes like those we saw in the Arctic, riding around on tracks with a total length of two kilometers for entertainment.

Before leaving, we had lunch in the house of one of the islanders whose walls were decorated with marine frescoes. When we asked her whether she would like to move off the island, our hostess replied unwaveringly:

Two "taxis" came for us in Bounty Bay. In the background are two aluminum lifeboats, a gift from New Zealand

"No, no way. We live well here. We don't think about leaving at all."

Speaking English with the same strange local accent, her husband, who limps a bit, added: "My hip hurts and on the next ship I'm going to hospital for an operation. But I'll be straight back."

His visit to the hospital will take at least a year because the supply ship from New Zealand—their only connection with the world—comes to Pitcairn just twice a year. When they say that things are great on the island and that they wouldn't swap with anyone, we have to believe them. The English tried twice to move the entire population, once to Tahiti, another time to New Zealand. The islanders returned from Tahiti in six months; from New Zealand it took them two years since it is farther away. They are resilient, these descendants of Fletcher Christian, persistent and obstinate, just like their forefathers.

---

1. Brac, one of the offshore islands of the Adriatic Sea, is about 100 miles southeast of Krajelvica where *Cigra* was built.

2. [Editor's Note: The only access to Turtle Bay is by dirt road. It would have been improbable for the soldiers to return the rifles to Cabo San Lucas.]

chapter ten

Into Chilean Waters

The island we next had to locate in the desolate region of the Pacific has many names. The present inhabitants call it Rapa Nui, but it acquired its name, Easter Island, from the Dutchman Roggeveen, who sighted it on Easter Sunday, 722. Since then it has been Easter Island for the English speaking world, and Isla de Pascua for the Chileans who annexed it in 888. For us it was just an island 1,117 miles from Pitcairn, or even to eight days of sailing.

nder full sail again

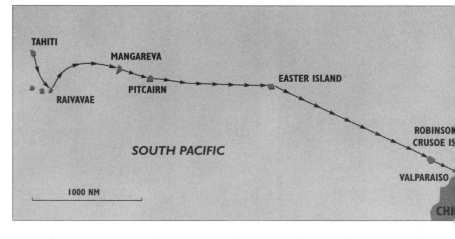

After our crew change in Tahiti, we had a few days of ocea
routine in which everyone did his tasks without complaining. V
slept as much as we could and gathered our strength for the ne
event.

During this time, Boris—whose nickname Palac mea
thumb—recalled his time as a student, serving us Pitcairn cabba;
in various ways. When he wasn't in the galley, he spent a good de
of time repairing the sail reef points or whipping ends on the r;
Cigra. He's quick at his work and was often a bit *too* quick for
team that had learned to leave certain tasks till the next day or tl
day after. He was impressively
calm and systematic.

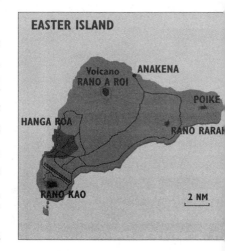

Dino's galley specialty was
bread. He had learned the technique of making pizza, and
when he didn't drop it on the
floor it was delicious. Dino is
someone we could really trust,
who forgets nothing and does
everything without a lot of talk.

The second "strong one"
from Dalmatia was Luka—a

future medical doctor who did odd jobs to pay his way through university. We became acquainted when I was renovating my flat and needed an assistant to help with the work. When it was completed, I sailed off to the Pacific, and he exclaimed to Tanja "He wasn't joking about leaving, was he!" because for two days, while we were carrying tiles to the roof, he kept asking me about the expedition.

In the end, he plucked up his courage and asked, "Could I go with you? What are the conditions?"

"There are plenty," I replied. "But you've already met some of them. I'll be happy to have you along."

He flew to Tahiti to meet us and, for a start, jumped into the sea and caught a ray with his spear gun. He's well educated, loves music and doesn't whine when he wakes up. During the Pacific voyage, Kruno and I fished along the rail of the boat, he on the port side, and I, with better equipment, along the starboard side—after all the skipper *is* the skipper! We each paid attention to our own line, pretending not to be interested in what the other was doing, casually waiting for the cry of "Fish! fish!" which— unfortunately—was seldom heard. We became the subject of the crew's derision but when we *did* catch a fish their tone changed at once:

"Here's a knife. Do you want me to clean the blood off the deck?"

At dusk, Kruno would roll up both lines and at dawn anyone who was still on his feet would cast them into the water again.

Although we can all cook quite well, Kruno was the best. He could turn anything that seemed totally out of the question into something edible, so his meals regularly ended with a round of applause and a "Bravo, chef!"

In his spare time he read the entire ship's library; he slept well, too, except when he forgot to shut the porthole and a wicked wave hit him in the face, or when I tipped him out of bed with a

Surviving the surf off Hanga Roa is a real challenge

gentle yell because the mainsail sheet fastening had sheared and I wanted him to repair it.

Because of his height (6' 5"), Branimir got the longest bunk. When he came down the narrow companionway into the saloon he had to make a move that someone christened the Murter Axel. He baked a loaf of bread that had a somewhat thicker crust than Dino's, but the center wasn't completely baked.

"Enjoy the grub," he told the crew. "This is the best bread I've ever baked. I believed him; it was his first try, and the first is always the best.

One day, with force of the wind propelling us along, the jib sheet block flew apart. After having improvised a great deal for two days, Branko said, "I'd like to repair

Harbor master's office shows light marine traffic

Moai at Anakena Bay were restored in 1978; their hats weigh over 10 tons

it. We'll drill new holes in these broken screws, cut in a thread, and there you are."

He was suggesting the impossible. This couldn't be done even in a workshop with a drill, new bits, and on steady ground, let alone on a boat. We bet three cases of beer on it and, as far as I was concerned, it could have been 20. There was absolutely no way!

Luckily, I was wrong. Branko is an incredibly skilled workman and, very soon, we had the sheets back in their place. On Easter Island, it was with pleasure that I looked around for *Cristal* beer.

Anchoring at Easter Island is just a shade easier than at Pitcairn. The island has two bays that offer marginal protection from the winds—Hanga Roa, off the village on its western side, and Anakena, on its northern side. Anakena is protected from southerlies; Hanga Roa from the prevailing south easterlies.

Thor Heyerdahl, famous for his Kon-Tiki project, came to Easter Island a few years after he had successfully sailed his raft across the Pacific. He was looking for proof to support his theory

Easter Island has about 1,000 of these moai, the largest weighing up to 300 tons

that the Pacific Islands had been colonized by people of South America.

A small freighter brought his big crew, lots of equipment and a team of researchers to the island. They remained here for eight months, struggling the entire time with the problem of anchoring. Depending on the wind, the ship would spend a few days in Anakena, returning to Hanga Roa again; and it takes about five or six hours of sailing between the two anchorages!

The island, which is renowned for its unusual sculptures, the *moai* and their ceremonial platforms called *ahu*—lies 2,300 miles from the mainland, a fact that drives some Chileans to distraction due to the difficulty of getting supplies. Although a jet airport was constructed in the 1980s this has not always improved the supply problem.

Twice a week a jet touches down here, unloads tourists, police, other officials, and electronics . . . but not potatoes or flour. These items come by freighter, unless it happens to capsize on the way, as one did just before we arrived; the ship sank two days after it had set out from Valparaiso and two members of its six-man crew were drowned. Some said it was because the vessel was too heavily loaded; others said it was due to the heavy storm.

We had not restocked in Polynesia dues to their high prices so, here at Rapa Nui, we lost our chance to stock up on provisions, and there was nothing left to do but find quick answers to the questions of who had built the great stone statues, the *moai,* and who was building a reed raft for a trans-Pacific expedition.

Our next destination, Mas a Tierra—the island closest to the Chilean coast (literally Closest to the Earth)—is the largest of the three islands in the Juan Fernandez Archipelago.

Fernandez was the first sailor to realize that the heavy winds and currents along the coast of South America, which made sail-

Gathering of reeds for construction of a 26-meter long raft to be used for a trans-Pacific expedition

The anchorage in Cumberland Bay at Robinson Crusoe Island

ing such a struggle, might not exist farther offshore. He proved his theory on one of his passages between Peru and Chile and discovered the archipelago, 200 miles offshore, which now bears his name.

Alexander Selkirk saw a similar scene but, unlike Fernandez, his visit was not due to exploration. After a dispute with his captain, Selkirk asked to be put off on what is now known as Robinson Crusoe Island with a gun, a little powder, a knife and the Bible. It is hard to say what he found most useful, but he survived for 52 months, enjoying fresh spring water, feeding on fruits and vegetables, birds, fish, and descendents of the goats originally left there by Fernandez.

Selkirk built two residences: one in a cave by the sea and another on the top of the mountain, a *mirador* (look-out point) from which he eventually spied the ship that rescued him.

Perfection in route-planning and the coordination of arrival times for new crew members reached its zenith on Robinson

A cave in the lava where Alexander Selkirk lived

Crusoe. When we anchored in Cumberland Bay and started to prepare breakfast, Palac took out the binoculars and sat on the bow searching the beach for Jadranko and Nikola—the two new members who were to join us.

Palac was looking in the wrong direction for his best friend. He should have been looking up at the sky, because our lads had flown the 15,000 kilometers from Zagreb and, at the very moment we were dropping anchor, they were landing on the island.

We bought lobsters —the most tempting

A fisherman found with a lobster less than 10cm (4 inches) is fined

product of the island—to celebrate a perfect meeting. The fishermen whose lobster pen we had emptied decided to share his earnings with everyone present. We left Robinson Crusoe with our souls singing, hugging some 30 or so islanders to the constant refrain of *Vive Chile! Viva Croatia!* And, when one of our lads let slip a *Viva Argentina,* we almost got a thrashing.

---

1. The only product of Robinson Crusoe Island is the lobster—*jasus frontali*—which will happily crawl into a lobster pot at a depth of 100 meters. It is sold to exclusive restaurants in Chile and Argentina and, occasionally, one gets a ride to New York by jet.

chapter eleven

To Patagonia

The crew for the Antarctic voyage gathered in Santiago de Chile. The same Air France plane that brought in five new crew members—four from Croatia and one from Slovenia—also took home the best crew of our entire voyage.

We took on Damjan in Valdivia the usual jumping-off port for an "assault" on the south. This town, with its German character and pretty women, is particularly lovely in the springtime when flowers are in bloom. Vegetables and fruit grow in abundance here and a boat can stock up on food and equipment at decent prices.

Located on the Calle-Calle River, Valdivia has two marinas and a small shipyard, owned by a German, that produces catamarans. We were able to repair the sail and buy a block, some glue, and 50 meters of line. This was as much as we could obtain because,

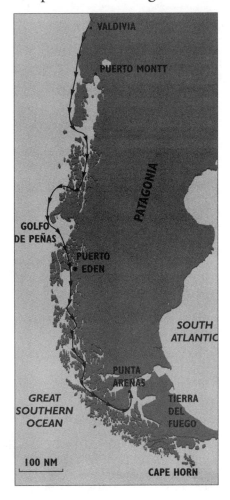

VALDIVIA

PUERTO MONTT

PATAGONIA

GOLFO
DE PEÑAS

PUERTO
EDEN

SOUTH
ATLANTIC

PUNTA
ARENAS

GREAT
SOUTHERN
OCEAN

TIERRA
DEL
FUEGO

100 NM

CAPE HORN

A labyrinth of a 1000 miles that is frequently cloud-covered

as in most of South America, the sailing industry is still in its infancy; the simplest trifles, like stainless steel screws, are unknown here.

Patagonia, which technically begins south of Valdivia and the island of Chiloe when you cross the Gulf of Peñas, is a region about 1,200 miles long where rain and snow fall almost continuously. Life is not easy even for animals, and the population per square kilometer is lower than that of the Sahara desert.

Aside from the city of Punta Arenas, on the Strait of Magellan, most of the population is employed by the Chilean Navy (Armada de Chile); the rest are fishermen

The last of the Alakalauf—once hardy hunters —had plenty of skins to keep them warm

who fish to their heart's
content but, in most
cases, have no idea of
where to sell their catch.
There are also about a
dozen descendants of the
original Indians—once
more numerous—who
lived here for almost
10,000 years, surviving
in the harsh climate
despite the shortage of

Winds of great velocities create interesting
tree patterns

food. In the middle of the 19th century, however, the white man
came to Patagonia, bringing with him sexually transmitted dis-
eases (among others), alcohol and tobacco, wiping out the Indian
population in just a hundred years.

With the wind behind us and the current carrying us along,
we sped southward in decent weather. We had come to Patagonia

The guanaco—a type of llama—can be seen on the eastern side of Patagonia at the best time of the year—early summer—and the route which had taken three or four days in 1989 in *Hir 3* now lasted just 24 hours. Help from the jib or genoa, along with the radar, allowed us to sail 160 to 180 miles a day in the labyrinth of channels where nature is beautiful but, due to cloud cover and mists, often cannot be appreciated.

Without a land mass to block them, the winds in the Great Southern Ocean roar continuously from west to east around Antarctica, sometimes attaining great velocities. Along 50° S latitude, there exists a divergent zone between the South Pacific and the Southern Ocean. As the winds and currents approach Madre de Dios Island along the coast of Chile, one component turns north toward the Galapagos (the Humboldt Current), the other component (the Falkland Current) turns south along the Andes and Cape Horn.

The question we faced in heading south along this coast was whether to sail during the day only—when the patterns of the wind on the water can be seen—and anchor every night, or to sail on through the dark, remaining constantly on the alert in unfamiliar and poorly-charted channels, worrying about jibing, having to reef the sails, or shake out the reefs as the wind decreased.

Anchoring every night may seem a simple solution, but because of the williwaws[1], constant watch must be kept in case the anchor drags over an unknown bottom. In this case, sleep is impossible. So, again, the captain must make a decision. I decided to sail whenever it was possible. This meant

Puerto Eden, near the entrance to the Patagonian Channels, has the only store for 400 miles

Making a run to shore for fresh water

that part of the crew could sleep soundly for hours, oblivious to the fact that we were sailing just 30 to 40 meters from shore, past rocks and obstacles shown (or perhaps not shown) on the chart.

My decision worked. We mastered the infamous Gulf of Peñas at night, and early in the morning we awakened the lighthouse keeper on San Pedro Island at the entrance to Canal Messier, the beginning of the Patagonian channels. The man was so confused that it took him a while to pull himself together. Twice he asked me to wait, which we interpreted as his hurriedly looking for socks and a pencil. We finally exchanged greetings, and just as I was going to tell him to have a good sleep, he called back: "Velero *Cigra* . . . " followed by static that wiped out part of his message, but we were able to guess that it referred to us.

"At about 1300 hours a submarine will be approaching from the opposite direction. Watch out. You might encounter it in Angostura Inglés [English Narrows]."

"On the surface or submerged?" I asked.

"Don't know. On the surface I suppose. Why would it dive?" asked the "controller" of shipping.

And, as predicted, at 1315 hours we met the ship of the Armada de Chile. After they introduced themselves over the radio, they asked how we would like to pass each other.

"Señor Capitán, rojo-rojo?"

"Si, rojo-rojo," I replied, meaning that we pass port-to-port so that we can see each other's red light.

We had already discovered that even the most up-to-date Chilean charts were inaccurate, having serious errors of up to two miles, so we had to be quite cautious through these channels.

At Puerto Bueno in Canal Sarmiento we managed to take on 200 liters of water from a waterfall that drains from a fresh-water lake. It was a bit yellowish from the muskeg, it was true, but after all, water is water.

Before entering the Strait of Magellan, at the end of Canal Smith, a large fishing vessel caught up with us. In a quick two-minute conversation we agreed to rendez-vous with them as soon as we came out of the narrows, and when we had rafted together we gave them a few packets of cigarettes. In turn, they gave us 10 kilos of cod and two squid, four kilos each.

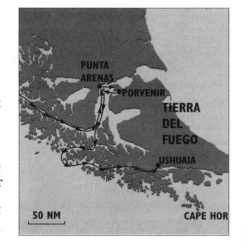

The fishing boat was 30 meters long with a crew of 25, which seemed too many to me, but they told us that for oceanic fishing many hands are needed.

In the Strait of Magellan we pulled into Borja Bay—one of the best anchorages in the strait where good anchor sites are difficult to find. Here, the williwaws are not so prevalent. A hundred years ago, Joshua Slocum in his sloop, *Spray,* had preferred this site. Following in his tradition and that of other boats, we nailed a sign with the name of our yacht, *Cigra,* to a tree.

Cabo Froward, the southernmost tip of the South American continent and the point where the Strait of Magellan turns north, is known for its heavy weather which can be as bad as that off Cape Horn. On the cliff above the cape stands a metal cross, recently erected and blessed by Pope

Cigra's aluminum sign, at the top of the tree, will last a lifetime

John himself who came—not by boat—but, like a divine shepherd dropped from the sky by helicopter. While we were toasting the end of the continent with the customary bottle of champagne, the Chilean navy's training ship—the four-masted *Esmerelda*—appeared on the horizon.

A short radio conversation established that the cadets had passed their qualifying tests by rounding Cape Horn four days earlier in a 50-knot gale and with only 40 percent of their sails. They had completed their training and were now on their way back to Valparaiso.

The duty officer was not exactly loquacious. At my insistence,

La Cueca, Chile's national dance performed on the pier. Behind the dancers Mr. and Mrs. Mijac waited to greet us

he found his skipper who told me that the following year *Esmeralda* would be in the Mediterranean, calling at Venice and after that at Split, in our country.

A few years earlier, I had received a letter from a certain Rudi Mijac in Punta Arenas, telling me that he regretted the fact that I hadn't stopped there in 1989 during the voyage of *Hir 3*, and asking me to send him two of my books. Rudi was the president of the Croatian Association of Punta Arenas and, after receiving my books, he wrote asking how much he owed me. I replied that he was in for two bottles of wine, which we would drink together the next time I visited Punta Arenas. Now the moment had come to collect, and we tied up in a city which has particular historical importance for Croatia, for it was here in southern Chile that the first Croatian sheepherders came to settle in the late 1800s.

I have a jaded opinion about the diplomatic staff of my country whom I have met around the world. But I do remember exceptions: Consul Sagrak in Ottawa, Kresimir Pirsal in Washington and, of course, Rudi Mijac, the honorary consul in Punta Arenas. It is with miraculous strength that he keeps together some 10,000 descendants of Croat exiles who live in Patagonia and Tierra del Fuego—a real skill, when you understand that unity is not one of our strong points.

At the urging of the consul, we crossed the strait from Punta Arenas to Porvenir, on the island of Tierra del Fuego, the region where most of the Croats settled. The entry into Porvenir Harbor is marginal due to heavy current and a shallow bar and, because we didn't have good charts, I wasn't crazy about making the trip. But Rudi couldn't be put off. He brought aboard new charts and a man in a captain's uniform.

"I would like to suggest," said Rudi, "if you don't mind, that the captain of the ferry who has done the Porvenir line for 18 years go with us."

A welcome ceremony for the first Croatian boat to visit Punta Arenas

I told him I didn't mind, but I wondered who was command-
ing the ferry.

"No one," he said. "We shut down the line. Today it is only
Cigra that is sailing to Tierra del Fuego."

Rudi took hold of a harmonica, Miro strummed the guitar,
and Damjan sang at the top of his lungs. I had no choice but to
go to Porvenir. I turned over the helm to Norberto Rodriguez,
who would sail to Antarctica with us, rounding out the international crew, and I led Griselda Mihovilovich—an amateur radio
operator from Punta Arenas, who, despite her name does not
know a word of Croatian—to the navigation station to show her
the equipment that had kept us in touch since Polynesia and
would keep us in touch with her all the way to Antarctica.

---

1. Williwaws are winds of high velocity that sweep down the sides of mountains.

chapter twelve

The End of the World

In the middle of the Strait of Magellan, south of Punta Arenas, the incident every modern sailor fears happened. Miro stood at the helm, completely helpless, his hands grasping a wheel that turned uselessly without resistance. Our steering gear had locked up, thoroughly and absolutely.

Cigra spun bow to the wind and headed for the shore of Dawson Island. Fortunately, the island was still 18 miles away, and although the drift was pushing us toward it, the wind was only 20 knots, and the sea was calm

I flew into the lazarette[1] where I expected I'd find the problem, all the while thinking about Dawson Island which, in recent Chilean history, was a place political prisoners were not gently treated.

Alan, who was close at hand and knew the most about our hydraulic system, pulled a screwdriver out from somewhere, tossed it to Jasminka and, in a second, explained what had to be done.

While his Croatian wasn't very good, Norberto understood immediately what a mess we were in and offered to help. Miro, who kicks himself right into gear in emergencies, organized the crew on deck and quickly lowered the sails.

Damjan got the video camera going and attempted to shoot the whole mess as I explained into his lens that I was using my finger to plug a 20-mm line in an attempt to stop fluid from leaking out of the system. If my finger hadn't been stuck in the line, I probably would have stuck it up his zoom lens. Since that day I've added a few new swear words to my vocabulary!

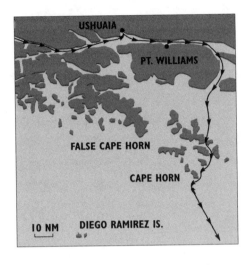

The problem was a leak in a coupling in the hydraulic system—suspect ever since the boat had been built. It might have held together if we hadn't installed a new auto pilot in Vancouver, where the experts had had to saw through the line when they installed it. It took fifty minutes to repair the line and pour in new fluid. We had saved the system! That night, I chose the best anchor site in Canal Moraleda, and we stayed there until we verified that the system was working.

After that, in an exciting night voyage, we sailed as far as Canal Beagle without stopping. I had switched off the depth sounder so the crew wouldn't get too distracted. (Since most of the canals are

Canal Beagle links the Atlantic to the Pacific

deep, I was worried less about the depths than about having them ruin their night vision.[2]) A rest stop in breathtaking Caleta Olla made up for the crew's anxiety about navigating without the depth sounder. This cove lies at the foot of the precipitous Cordillera Darwin with Holland Glacier rumbling ponderously into the sea and the winding, icy Rio Italia dropping noisily into the water.

It was a pity that

At the foot of magnificent Holland Glacier

We heeded the warning

because of the *marea roja* [red tide] we weren't able to eat the mussels that had once been the mainstay of the Ona, Yaghan and Alakaluf tribes. The poisons generated by this phenomenon cause PSP (paralytic shellfish poisoning), immediately affecting the nervous system. We had been warned about it by radio early on, and learned that one French yachtsman in Puerto Williams had died from the illness while many others had needed months of treatment.

It is difficult to understand how—in an area where there is no pollution, no industry, no oil—a condition as toxic as the *marea*

The glaciers in Canal Beagle made a lasting impression on our crew

roja can exist.[3] We had sailed thousands of miles only to find ourselves unable to eat a single one of the *cholgas* that grow in abundance on the beaches and rocks of Patagonia.

We sailed into Ushuaia, the town which bills itself as *Fin del
Mundo*—the end of the world—where tourism is in full swing.
Slender masts rose in the wide, shallow and well-protected bay;
there were at least 10 yachts here, which in South America means
high tourist season. The French, the most prolific sailors in world
terms, are usually in the forefront. In addition, there was one
Canadian, one American, and two German boats.

I soon found my acquaintances of seven years earlier. Oleg now
had teen-age children; Jean Paul was off chartering; Guillermo was
still working on the 9-meter boat he had started in 1989!

It is a strange society that comes together here in Ushuaia.
Sailors live year-round on their boats, exposed to the ceaselessly
blowing winds. Often they can't even land their dinghies on shore,
and when they do, they always get drenched. Oleg's children were
enrolled in a correspondence school and his wife looked as if she

High tourist season in Ushuaia

has fled from a sanatorium for pulmonary ailments. He had sold his first boat, *Kotic I*, to a Frenchman, a strange and dirty character whose crew was a curious individual with several characters embodied in one. Housekeeper, mistress, and first mate, she was an attractive black African woman, with mysterious genes that drove her to the cold of Antarctica every year.

Since 1989, Jean-Paul had built a house, but Guillermo had lost his in a fire. He gave us a slightly burned chart of the Falklands for the continuation of our voyage, adding with a bitter smile, "It's the only thing I managed to save."

The skippers of these boats who charter out of Ushuaia pay taxes to no one. They are careful not to irritate the Chilean navy in Puerto Williams because they are the only officials who can give permission to sail around Cape Horn. The charterers cheat three countries equally—their own country, Chile, and Argentina—but because there are not many of them, these technicalities are overlooked. People at the end of the world are happy about their contribution to the tourist industry.

A trip to Cape Horn on a charter boat from Ushuaia costs about $2,000 per person; to Antarctica, $6,000 to $7,000. The best known of the charterers is Poncet who has lived with his wife in this hostile environment for 15 years. He knows South Georgia, Antarctics, the South Shetlands and other "destinations" in the Southern Ocean better than he does the Côte d'Azur, and he has made so much money that, a few years ago, he was able to buy Beaver Island in the Falklands.

Cigra was a much larger and incomparably better yacht than all the others in Ushuaia, so I made a proposal to Miro: "After Antarctica, we'll go home. Since we promised to return to Kraljevica, we have to keep our word. But after that, what can stop us from coming back and earning $60,000? A few months of rather difficult but highly profitable sailing. Then . . . skiing on the southernmost *piste* in the world."

Miro was taken by surprise, but his answer was quick and concise, "Virovitica." ["You're crazy!"]

So that was it. We missed out on the chance of a lifetime!

From Ushuaia to Puerto Williams, the southernmost town in Chile, we had a little race with two other yachts. One, the *Darwin Sound,* was a nice boat, but the skipper wasn't very likable, and a woman to boot. In Ushuaia we hadn't been able to switch on the radio without having her answer, and she soon got on everyone's nerves. In the *Prefectura Naval* they were happy when she received her papers to proceed with her voyage.

We liked the crew of the second yacht, *Northanger,* who had transited the Northwest Passage in two hard years in 1988–1989. They ran aground in Peel Sound, then got stuck near Hershel Island with serious problems. They failed to master the last 400 miles to Barrow Point during the first season—the owner of the boat died in a climbing accident during the attempt. *Northanger's* current owner, Greg Landreth, who was part of the original crew,

The southernmost town of Chile is a naval base

Cigra moored off Horn Island, perilously close to shore

managed to complete the Northwest Passage the following summer.

Our three boats tied up at the world's most southerly marina, Club Nautico de Puerto Williams, the "waiting room" for travellers to Cape Horn. Although you can get to this magical point by an-

Going ashore on Horn Island is a risky business

other route, the Chilean authorities order everyone to check in here, first, so they can inspect the boats and issue their papers or . . . perhaps deny them.

The procedure usually lasts three or four days, because the blessing must come from the Commandante in Valparaiso. Although the naval authorities in Puerto Williams were courteous, I knew what the officials were like at headquarters in

Valparaiso. They had caused us a fair amount of damage and trouble, and when I gave the duty officer a piece of my mind, they forbade us to leave. Until the high command made up its mind to meet with us in the Commandante's office, we had had plenty of time to go sightseeing in Santiago as well as in Viña del Mar, Chile's riviera and most popular resort city.

I had rounded Cape Horn with Ozren in *Hir 3* without either notification or permission but this time, since some of the Antarctic bases belong to Chile, it was a good idea for us to abide by regulations, especially since we had Norberto, a Chilean national, on board.

We received our permission several days later and set sail from Puerto Williams. Cape Horn came into sight around 0500 on December 19, 1996. That night I slept only until midnight and after that, with the duty helmsman, I took *Cigra* through the labyrinth of Wollaston Channel, recalling the days in 1989, when I had sailed through these desolate waters with Ozren Bakrac. At that time, the Horn was our aim; this time it was just a way-station.

To keep things exciting and to prevent the trip from becoming too easy, I decided to land on Horn Island[4], possible in theory but not easy or without danger. The weather was all right, but the wind was blowing from the wrong quarter—the east. The prevailing winds off the Horn are from the west and southwest, and although an east wind is good for sailing from the Atlantic into the Pacific, it is *not* good for anchoring in Horn island's only accessible bay. The Chilean Navy uses this bay to supply the keepers of the island, and I had to do some hard negotiating to convince them to let us tie to their buoy.[5]

For an hour I weighed our chances of getting ashore, then finally decided to take the risk. "Let's do it. It's now or never!"

Miro took the first group ashore at 0710. They rowed through the kelp, and remained on the island for 70 minutes; since it wasn't raining at the time they managed to shoot some good footage.

The rest of us set out after they returned. A sailor with a dog was waiting on the beach to lead us to the top of the island where two other officials met us. Wooden stairs have been built to the hut at the top because it is impossible to climb the island's steep, rocky face.

One of the sailors was listening to the radio; the other sat behind a large table, selling Cape Horn souvenirs at astronomical prices and putting an offi-

Wooden stairs lead to the top of Horn Island

The albatross monument, installed in 1992, is inscribed *A los intrepidos navegantes que han surcado estes aguas* [To the intrepid sailors who have navigated these seas]

cial stamp on anything we wanted him to. We remained on the
island for an hour, talking to
them and visiting the little
chapel. "The wind blows violently here," they told us. I felt like
replying, "You can't be serious!"

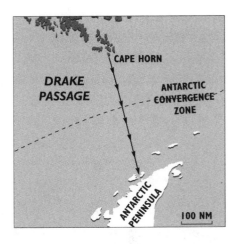

The sailor in charge told us,
"On average, our anemometer
registers about 35 knots but, at
intervals of three or four days,
we measure 60 to 80 knots. In winter it's considerably calmer, but
when it blows, it's really vile."

"How bad?" I asked him.

"Often over a hundred, and sometimes up to 150 knots, with
temperatures of about -15°C [17°F]. That's when we start worrying about our hut."

Justifiably, I thought. The hut looked so primitive and poorly
constructed that it didn't inspire much confidence. We said goodbye to the sailors and headed back down to shore. The sailor with
the dog warned us about the kelp. "If you get tangled up in it, we
will have to call for a helicopter. We don't have a boat here."

Half an hour later we
sailed across the meridian
that marks the official
boundary between the
Atlantic and the Pacific.
We drank a glass of cham-
pagne, had our photos
taken in the rain, and
turned our heading to a
new course of 167°.

Three sailors and a dog man this hut for
three months at a time

Saying goodbye to Cape Horn

Cape Horn quickly vanished in the rain and fog as one of the sailors came on the radio:
"In thirty minutes, call our base on Diego Ramirez.⁶

---

1. Lazarette: a compartment at the stern of the boat

2. Looking at any light within the pilothouse, including the numbers on a depth meter, ruins night vision and can distract a helmsman from his critical duty of watching the boat's course.

3. Red tide is caused by an "explosion" of toxic, naturally-occurring microscopic plankton caused by environmental conditions such as warm surface temperatures, high nutrient content, low salinity and calm seas. The phenomenon occurs in Southeast Alaska, as well as in Patagonia, particularly in summer.

4. The world's most famous cape is really an island. The Dutchmen, Schouten and le Maire, who sighted the island in 1616, named it Cape Hoorn, after the town of their chief financial backer. They did not realize at the time that the cape was an island.

5. It required an hour or two of diplomacy on my part to convince the Navy to give us permission to go ashore. If they had said "no", we would not have gone ashore.

6. Cape Horn is not the southernmost point of South America. There is always something worse than the worst! In this case, it is Diego Ramirez Island, where three "captive" Chilean sailors live. Although not as famous as Cape Horn, it is just as dangerous. A boat can break up here just as well as off the Horn. After all, that's how the island of Diego Ramirez was discovered.

chapter thirteen

The White Continent

When Francis Drake, the brilliant buccaneer and sailor, first sailed into the Strait of Magellan in 1578, he made the 364-mile passage from the Atlantic to the Pacific in just 16 days.

The Pacific Ocean is not often peaceful in the vicinity of Tierra del Fuego and Cape Horn, however, and when the intrepid Englishman and his fleet headed out into the ocean from the western side of the Strait, they encountered an ugly storm that blew them somewhere to the south, thus discovering the passage that bears Drake's name.

At full speed through Drake Passage!

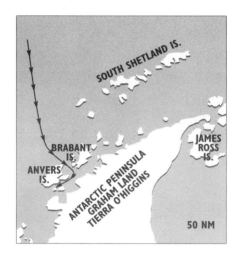

World maritime literature is unanimous: Drake Passage is the most dangerous navigational zone on the face of the Earth. In the passage between Antarctica and Tierra del Fuego, with an average distance of about 500 miles, anything can happen. Here, three essentially different systems—the Pacific, the Atlantic and the Antarctic—meet and collide violently. Each has different current speeds, temperatures, water density and salinity. From the west, masses of moist air move rapidly above the water, and cyclonic storms come one after another like beads on a necklace. One barrier to these storms is the Andes; another is Antarctica, the highest continent in the world. When the air masses are deflected by these two continents, they converge in the center of Drake Passage, and chaos on the high seas is inevitable. If fog, rain and an occasional iceberg manage to find their way

Reefing the mizzen in gale-force winds requires four men working ten minutes

into all this, an exciting adventure is guaranteed.

The worst conditions prevail off Cape Horn and a hundred miles to the southwest. After that, every mile south, closer to Antarctica, is a mile closer to better weather, longer days, and safer sailing.

Low temperatures in summer, let alone winter, pretty well exhaust a crew; the ice threatens a boat's stability, and the distance from civilization stirs up anxiety in every maritime soul.

Our tactics for this exposed area were based on a simple philosophy: to sail on at all possible speed, minimizing our exposure to weather and seas. We would push the boat and crew to the limit, given the conditions, but not to the point where sails rip, lines break and the crew suffers from lack of sleep. This is why we had spent so much money on line and blocks in Valdivia and the reason I wanted nine crew members and two sets of sails—to get to our goal safely and to return.

We spotted Antarctica through the mist, high, white and unreal

Sailing 509 miles in a straight line we spotted Antarctica 87 hours after putting Cape Horn behind our stern. Through fog and with bad visibility, we saw our target in the right place—the passage between Brabant and Anvers islands that leads to small Melchior archipelago and on into Gerlache Channel. The islands were there right in front of us—high and white, quite unreal compared to what I had imagined.

When we touched the first piece of Antarctic ice with our bow, I immediately radioed Griselda in Punta Arenas: "Radio Magellanes, *Cigra!*" and in ten minutes she put me in contact with Zagreb.

"We have arrived in Antarctica!" I told my wife, Tanja, giving her a brief report on everything that had happened and asking her to call Engineer Walter in Kraljevica to tell him we had arrived.

"Do you have any other messages for him?"

"None. Just that. He knows how much this goal means to me, and I know what it means to him and everyone who believes in us. That's all."

Antarctica, the White Continent, the seventh continent, is an almost unknown part of the world. Until 1948, when the Americans launched an impressive expedition—Operation High Jump, under the command of Admiral Richard Byrd—no one had known what the entire continent looked like.

Bird, who was well qualified for

This aggressive leopard seal was the only border guard to greet us

the command of Operation High Jump, had flown over the South Pole in a plane in 1929 and endured the harsh Antarctic winter of 1935 alone in a cabin covered with snow. But for Operation High Jump, the most ambitious expedition ever mounted to Antarctica, he was not alone; as many as 4,700 men, 13 ships, and 24 air-

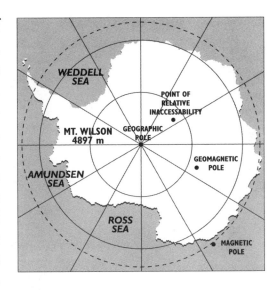

craft were involved in the expedition; nothing similar had ever been attempted. That and ensuing expeditions have given us a chart of Antarctica and a lot of new knowledge about it.

Antarctica is larger than Europe and Australia and about half the size of Africa. Its 14 million square kilometers are, on average, the highest on Earth. The mean elevation of the continent is 2,050 meters, compared to 600 meters for the rest of the world. Antarctica has four poles.[1] It is always covered in snow and ice and in summer, only two per cent of the land is free of ice. This came as a surprise to those of us who had experienced the Arctic where large portions of the ice melt in summer. In comparison to Antarctica, Greenland's massive ice cap is like a single ridge on the White Continent.

Here, where Antarctic ice makes up nine percent of all the world's frozen water, it is difficult to distinguish the land from the icebergs. If all the ice in Antarctica were to melt—and we may be well on the way to seeing it happen —the level of the world's oceans would rise by about 70 meters. Despite all that we know about this place the icy continent still hides a great many mysteries.

Excited by all this new knowledge, we sailed into the bay of Port Lockroy where the remains of the British Arctic Survey base (BAS) can still be seen. As we sailed by the living quarters of the former base, we saw two men at the door. We anchored in a depth of 15 meter with no chance of tying a stern line to shore as

Endurance trapped in Antarctic ice in 1914[2]

Robert Falcon Scott's race to the South Pole against Amundsen ended tragically. Here, (center) he celebrates his last birthday in the British base at McMurdo Sound

our acquaintances in Ushuaia had suggested. Personally, I had been dubious about this technique, because we hadn't been able to pull it off in *Hir 3* which was smaller and lighter, let alone with *Cigra's* fifty tons. Besides, since tons of snow and ice crash into the sea from the coast every ten minutes, it's best not to be near shore.

We had been surprised to see the people at the base, and when we were anchored, we called them on the radio.

"Welcome, *Cigra!*" they answered.

The Gentoo penguins attain a height of about 3 feet and weigh an average of 13 lbs.

Their pronunciation of *Cigra* was good, but when we asked for an explanation, we couldn't get though—their batteries had run out.

The next morning, Norman, one of the two men, cleared things up:

"Two years ago I had a girlfriend in Zagreb, and the last time I visited her, I noticed a tram painted with the emblems and logos of your expedition. I remembered the name of your yacht and I was expecting you."

I have always known that it was a small world and now I had proof.

"I'm glad that you have finally come to the Antarctic," he said.

"How did you find the Arctic?"
Quite incredible, we told him.

We had a look around the island and the bay, and enjoyed watching and photographing the penguins. These incredible birds have excellent thermal insulation. A thick layer of fat under its feathers—a third of its body weight—serves as a food reserve.

It was a sunny Christmas Eve and I was on galley watch. My duty was to catch some fish. When this came to nothing, I decided to prepare *pasticada a la Antarctica* with meat from Croatia we had in the freezer. Jasminka took pity on me and made potato gnocchi. For the sauce, instead of Dalmatian *prosek³*, I used a sweet Chilean wine that Mijac, our Croatian Consul in Punta Arenas had given us. The crew said dinner was excellent. Damjan and Alan had decorated the saloon beautifully and Berislav skillfully drew a banner with Christmas greetings and designed a *Feliz Navidad* for Norberto. I was happy. Not every day is Christmas— especially in Antarctica!

---

1. The Geographical South Pole; Magnetic Pole; Geomagnetic South Pole; Pole of Relative Inaccessibility.

2. Sir Earnest Shackleton was the first to set off to try to conquer the South Pole. When he reached the magnetic pole, he set off for the geographical pole, reaching 87° 23' South, just 180 kilometers short of the goal. In a 2,000-kilometer-long march he experimented with ponies, two years before Scott determined that they were not suitable for Antarctic conditions. He has gone down in the history of Antarctica as one of the bravest and most persistent of explorers. His ship *Endurance* was trapped in the ice in the Weddel Sea, and he and his crew remained on board for 10 months, doing 573 miles, before the ship was ultimately crushed by the ice. Under Shackleton's superb leadership, they took to the lifeboats and managed to reach Elephant Isle in the South Shetlands. In an open boat, Shackleton sailed 800 miles to South Georgia for help. Thus in 1914, the year World War I broke out, the plan for a brave Englishman to walk from one side of Antarctica to the other and leave his flag at the pole came to nothing.

3. Prosek (pronounced prosheck) is a sweet Croatian white wine aged in oak barrels. Pasticada is a beef dish marinated in oil and lemon and seasoned with cloves, bacon, garlic and onion and simmered in Prosek for several hours.

chapter fourteen

Farewell to Antarctica

A treaty signed by twelve nations at a conference in Washington in 1959 set up the basic rules of conduct that put territorial claims to Antarctica in abeyance. This meant that when *Cigra* sailed into the White Continent, we did not have to draw up a crew list or lose half a day talking with port authorities.

To visit Antarctica, you don't need a visa or passport; there are no customs or immigration officials. Theoretically, you could build a house and live a "hassle-free" life if you had the money to hire a freighter and have your materials shipped down—and if you could endure the climate. But the Antarctic is too rare a land for it to be that easy. Some thirty nations have been laying claim to the continent for years, and every day there are more that want to become signatories to the Antarctic treaty.

Chile drew its own slice of the cake on the map of Antarctica and calls it Antarctica Chilena; Argentina calls its part Antarctica Argentina. That their interests overlap, as do the slices of the cake, bothers no one. On the other side of the continent, similar sketches have been made by the Russians, the Americans, the

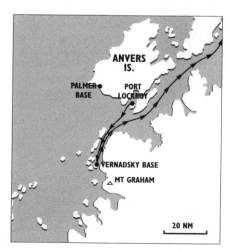

127

New Zealanders, the Australians, and the French, among others.

Great Britain "reserves" for itself that portion which is south of the Falklands and, just in case, it builds bases all over the continent. Our new friend, Norman, in Port Lockroy, was not there just to sell postcards to rich tourists who pay top dollar to come and watch penguins sitting on their eggs. He is also keeping an eye on British "property."

We travelled toward our target, Vernadsky Base, formerly the British base, Faraday, by way of spectacular Canal Le Maire which is bordered on one side by Graham Land and on the other by Booth, Hovgaard and Peterman islands. In Lockroy we had been informed that this channel was crammed with ice, and we heard similar information from the commander of a Russian passenger ship that had passed us.

It was fortunate that we already knew the different criteria for ice and had headed south without a lot of discussion, passing the old, abandoned Argentine base on Peterman Island. We had been

Narrow Le Maire Strait is impassable ten months a year

Cigra glides past an iceberg

told in Ushuaia that we could use it to winter in, but it didn't seem safe because, in the center of the bay where we would have had to anchor, we found an enormous ice floe, and the bay itself was exposed to the northeast wind.

It was about 2200 hours when we arrived at Vernadsky (formerly Faraday after a British physicist). This was a base the English had abandoned in 1995 for a new, larger and more expensive facility on Adelaide Island. The story we heard was that in a gentlemanly deal, the British gave the complete base, with all its equipment, computers and measurement instruments, to the Ukrainians. They filled the tanks with fuel and the shelves with spare parts; they lubricated the lathes and mixed oil with gasoline for the Seagull outboards. And this was not all; they assigned three instructors to teach the Ukrainians everything about the base and its equipment as well as instruct them in Arctic survival. They supposedly even translated the fire drill instructions into Ukrainian, without charging a dollar for it. The sole obligation of

Pushing through the ice to the Ukrainian's Vernadsky Base

the new owners was to supply the British Arctic Survey with copies of all their measurements and research.

I had pre-arranged a radio schedule at 2200 hours with Griselda, our Punta Arenas ham contact. This coincided with our arrival at Vernadsky, so I called and asked her to wait. We still had 280 meters of sheet ice to break through in Meeck Channel before we could anchor, but our Arctic "eyes" found this ice to be an easy nut to crack.

It was still daylight in the midnight hours, and, to the excited cheering of the Ukrainians—we were the first humans they had seen in 11 months— we pushed our way through to the base and anchored in our

Vernadsky Base (formerly the British Base Faraday)

own iced-over wake. First aboard was a man, whom we later learned was a glaciologist of world renown with 20 years experience in Antarctica. He tromped around *Cigra* on skis, taking photos, and occasionally entertaining us by shooing

Dr. Milinevski of Kiev University with his Dobson instrument for measuring ultra-violet light

away the penguins as we were breaking the ice.

Vernadsky Base is named after a famous professor of Kiev University. The men who live and work here collect meteorological data and measure UV radiation, magnetic and seismic changes, and the quality of the spread of radio waves. They also photograph the sky and polar light, keep an eye on the state of the ice and monitor the speed of iceberg movement. Their sole link with the world is via Inmarsat but, because of its high cost, they use it just once a week when the radio operator sends out email with essential messages only. For 12 months of total isolation they are paid $500 a month (only slightly higher than in Kiev)—all for the good of science.

The group of likeable young scientists, along with their leader, Dr. Genady Milinevski of Kiev University, received us amicably waiting on skis and dressed in our honor in suits, white shirts and ties.

One of the scientists was a Russian which surprised us, for Russians and Ukrainians get along about as well as Croats and Serbs. This handy fellow had made a sauna from odds and ends in the carpenter's workshop, and we sweated out the dirt we had produced over the past two weeks. Then, with steaming heads, we jumped into the chilly sea.

In celebration of our visit, Dr. Milinevski relaxed somewhat and allowed his team (who were counting the days till the ship from Odessa would bring new crew) to treat us to the specialty of the house—vodka made right on their Antarctic base. Although each member of the base carefully guards his own secret recipe, we managed to discover that the main ingredients

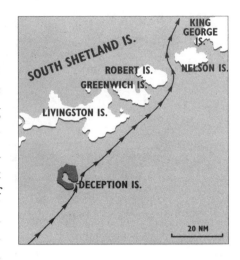

are: sugar, raisins, potatoes, yeast, wheat, surgical alcohol, rice, ice water, and desalinated water . . . Imagination and free time work wonders!

To guard against pollution and the build up of rubbish, smoking is forbidden, both inside and outside of the base buildings except in the clubhouse where the British left them a few games for entertainment, a wooden bar, and a few photographs of Britain's "illustrious" past.

We had planned to say our farewell to Antarctica from Deception Island, one of the South Shetlands, where one of the two active volcanoes on the continent is found, so we sailed north.[1]

Celebrating aboard *Cigra* with the Ukrainians

Although geographically separated from the tip of Antarctica, the Shetland Islands are normally included in the description of the continent.

For over a hundred years, Deception Island was the largest whaling station in Antarctica. Discovered in 1819 by the English navigator, Captain William Smith, the waters around Deception were found to have large colonies of fur seals. The increasingly profitable market for fur and oil attracted countless ships to the region and, within just two years, more than 300,000 seals had been slaughtered, nearly decimating the population.

After that began the hunt for whales which lasted nearly a century, a "success" shown by figures as recent as 1937-38, when between 50,000 and 60,000 whales were slaughtered.

It is hard to say how long this slaughter would have lasted— ecological awareness alone might not have broken the pattern. But something just as serious stopped it. During the early days of World War II, there was the fear that the Germans would take Deception Island as a supply base for their ships and infamous U-boats. However, the British fleet entered the crater and destroyed the station thus bringing peace to the Antarctic whales, at least.

After the war, three powers, Chile, Argentina and Britain, built bases on Deception Island. Each one intended to make claims to the property, claims that have been blunted by the Washington treaty. While politicians in their offices were busy trying to outwit one another, the crews on the bases lived together at the edge of the world in hazardous conditions and began to help each other. They made an agreement concerning leadership, because it was obvious that if something serious went wrong, they would need to cooperate and someone would have to be in charge.

The problem was resolved sportingly. Each year a football tournament was played; the winner then took charge and his base became the logistical center for the following year.

The harmony on Deception was ultimately cut short not by politics but by a volcanic eruption that occurred December 4, 1967, forcing the evacuation of all crews. Since then, Port Foster—the official name of the crater—has been left exclusively to casual travellers and sailors.

Cigra entered the crater through Neptune's Bellows, a 250-meter-wide passage. If there had been a banner hanging above the entire entrance inscribed with Dante's verse, *Lasciate ogni speranza voi ch'entrate* [Who enters here abandons all hope], I would not have been surprised. Entry into hell, itself, could not have looked very different.

To avoid a sunken whaler which lies in the center of Neptune's Bellows, we entered the crater along its northern shore; steam, fog and mist surrounded us, and a "lake" of three to five miles wide lay in front. Although it appeared to be a well-protected anchorage, fierce williwaws sweep down from the steep slopes above, constantly changing direction. In addition, depths in the bay range from 40 to 90 meters (130 to 290 feet).

The entrance to Neptune's Bellows is "guarded" by this natural obelisk

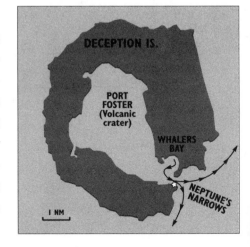

Whale bones preserved under a layer of sand

Although the sailing directions recommended against it, we anchored in Balleñeros Bay which, as the name suggests, used to be the whaling base. When both of our anchors were secure in the sand in the immediate vicinity of shore, I was convinced they would hold, especially if we hooked some sunken ship or part of an iron construction that had ended up under the sea in a previous earthquake or volcanic eruption; but then, we could have a serious problem.

A greedy skua liked our biscuits

The view from the edge of hell's crater

Alan read my thoughts and added quietly: "If the anchor gets stuck, we can dive to these depths. The equipment is all ready."

I was grateful for his words, and Miro quickly concluded the officers' meeting with, "Well, we're not going to winter here. Just one night, and if necessary . . . it wouldn't be the first time we had to dive and sail out in the middle of the night."

Bor looked at conditions and said, "I'd rather not go ashore. It looks too depressing."

Nevertheless, we all took a stroll along the black sandy beach where steam rose all around. Here and there, we saw the occasional remains of a whaler's boat, and whale ribs protruding from the sand. In some places, the temperature of the sea was above 30°C (86°F).

Penguins waddling along the beach jumped all the time trying to avoid the steam vents; with their layer of fat as insulation and their low body temperature, heat does not suit them.[2] Only the albatross and skua which like warm earth and a turbid atmosphere, seemed to enjoy the eerie atmosphere. We were all quite moved.

In the morning we raised both anchors, and shook ash, soot and ice crystals from the sails. This was a strange place, but at

More ice to go through before *Cigra* was safe again

least the wind was on our side. As we sailed away, most of the crew enjoyed the panorama of the South Shetlands, while Berislav and I spent the entire day repairing the galley pump.

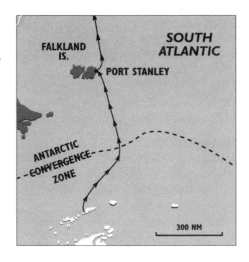

Miro and the crew took *Cigra* through Nelson Strait, and we were once again in Drake Passage, exposed to all winds. When they reported to me that there was no longer any ice ahead of us, I went on deck and breathed a sigh of relief.

At last! Two goals accomplished: the pump was repaired and draining the sink again; but most important, our mission was complete.

Farewell Arctic! Farewell Antarctica! We would still have 10,163 miles to go—to sail across Drake Passage, call at the Falkland Islands, then head north across the South Atlantic to the Adriatic and our homeport of Kraljevica, the town where *Cigra* was born. After 37 months and 40,000 miles, our voyage around the Americas from top to bottom would end successfully.

---

1. Deception Island is interesting in many ways, starting with the fact that a boat can sail right into its crater. Its name in English has a distinctly negative connotation, but we were told that in Spanish it means surprise, implying perhaps a warning or need for special care.

2. Eight or nine species of penguin live in Antarctica. Their spindle-shaped bodies, excellent hydrodynamic lines and wing movements are the same as that of a bird that can fly; they hurtle through the water at speeds of up to 16 knots. On land, they raise their wings to let the wind cool them off.

Afterword

Since our return, people have often asked me: How did you ever organize this whole undertaking? How did you manage to build the boat? Where did you get the financing? My answer is that people believed in us and in our project. The building of *Cigra*, the procurement of our equipment, and the financing of the entire project were made possible by people whose acquaintance I had made in recent years. Accomplished on the basis of mutual trust, it was a sensitive and long-term process during which certain people saw something new and exciting in our ideas and actions. They supported *us*. *We* made it happen.

Not least of those involved were the members of the crew who, once we were underway, rotated throughout the voyage. All told, there were 37 of us; men and women, Croats and foreigners. Most carried out all their responsibilities with care, making a contribution to the safety of the voyage, to the good humor that prevailed on board, and to the realization of the project.

There were a few problems, of course, but these were trifles—normal sparks that fly between people who live in a confined space and under abnormal conditions. What is important to me is that never, not at a single moment, was anyone's safety or the safety of *Cigra* put at risk due to fatigue or fleeting bad tempers. Everyone fulfilled his or her challenging tasks with concentration and superb discipline. Responsibility for the boat, the equipment, other people's lives and basic order, was kept at a very high level all three years of the voyage.

I have to admit that, with four members of the crew, I didn't have such good luck. Statisticians would say that a 10 percent attrition rate is not bad. However, looking at things in another way, if there are five in a crew and one member does not function properly, that is 20 percent, a much higher failure rate than is acceptable.

Overall, though, I was quite pleased with the individuals who made up *Cigra's* crew. No one received a scratch, let alone anything more serious. But, most important of all, the crew all made it safely home to their parents, wives, companions and friends. We accomplished this by having people take each others' places every few months.

For Miro and me this had advantages and disadvantages. The good was that we came to life when new blood showed up—the recruits were full of strength and desires of their own, each with different interests and a new way of looking at things. The bad side was that it usually took several weeks to teach them seamanship. Then, at last, when they had mastered the most complex actions on deck in a stormy night—taking in a reef or lowering the mainsail, for example—they had to return home. But, in the end, the way we organized the voyage by having the crew rotate turned out to be correct. Everyone had just the right amount of time to make his or her unique contribution to the project.

Many people understood and helped make our Arctic-Antarctic Expedition a reality. It is vital that, when you set off on such a voyage you have the support and encouragement of those close to you. Going to sea should not be taken as an escape from real life but as a life-affirming change that enhances your experiences, teaches you something and prepares you for a better quality of life in the future.

Personally, as I look back over this ambitious undertaking, I think the key to our success was our determination to complete the project we had envisioned, without a single thing being left undone. No one likes incompleteness, even if it is caused by something out of your control. When others have confidence in you they expect success, not disappointment, and in our case, this was a lien on the future, a burden that sat heavily on our shoulders until *Cigra* returned to her home port.

I hope that the multitude of good people who put their hard work and reputations into the project are more than satisfied with what we accomplished. I thank them one and all for their belief in us and their support. If, together, we created some new adventures and memories, then the effort was worth it. The desire to accomplish this trip was something we inherited from our long-standing history of Croatian seamanship. I believe that, as a result of this voyage, we created a legacy for future generations, for lovers of the sea and, ultimately, for ourselves.

Editor's note: *Cigra,* now berthed in Biograd on Croatia's central coast, belongs to the Club Nautika founded a number of years ago by the author. The ketch is available to its members for cruisings.

Principals of the Expedition

Mladen Sutej (born 1945), from Zagreb, mechanical engineer. He has been sailing for more than four decades, with 150,000 miles of experience. He was the first Croat to sail the Atlantic single-handedly (1983, Las Palmas to Barbados, 2850 NM in 22 days and 19 hours). His second solo voyage was in the Pacific in 1989, from Robinson Crusoe Island to Rangiroa Atoll in Polynesia, a 4236-mile voy-

age completed in 34 days and 5 hours; with Ozren Bakrac he rounded Cape Horn that same year. All this took place on the 10-meter fiberglass yacht *Hir 3*. Mladen has written two books: *The Challenge of the Atlantic* (1984) and *Round Cape Horn by Yacht* (1991). He organized the first sailing school in the Adriatic, and ran it for eight years. Most of those taking part in the Arctic-Antarctic Expedition were actually some of the best to pass through the school, which has been attended by some 1,600 people from all over Europe.

Miroslav (Miro) Muhek (born 1958), aeronautical engineer, was born in Virovitica and lives in Zagreb. He took part in the project from day one. During the construction of *Cigra* he took care, among other things, of the wiring, the electronics and the installation of all machines running on electricity. Miro is the only one to have sailed the entire route and is, without doubt, one of the people to be credited most with the success of the entire project.

Tatjana (Tanja) Tetus-Sutej (born 1963), architect from Zagreb, devised and drew the designs for the entire interior of *Cigra,* She also designed the emblems and symbols of the club and the expedition, including the logo along the bow of *Cigra* in which a bird gradually turns into a sailboat. When not on board, Tanja undertook rather complex problems in Zagreb, obtained air tickets and looked after crew members on departure, found sponsors, spare parts and a lot more.

Igor Milkovic (born 1963) from Zagreb, mechanical engineer. He, too, was a founder of the nautical club and took part in the operation from day one. Igor spent all ten months of Cigra's construction in Kraljevica and was the main coordinator of the work. He made an invaluable contribution.

Dubravko Belan (born 1952) from Karlovac was one of the prime movers of the entire project. He took care of day-to-day operational problems in the shipyard. During the first year of the voyage, he served as first mate.

Alan Smojver (born 1968) from Zagreb, is a mechanical and marine engineer. While *Cigra* was being built, all calculations went through his hands, and he drew hundreds of plans and workshop drawings.

CREW MEMBERS

Jelena Belamaric (1965), Zagreb, biologist
Damjan Brajnik (1951), Ljubljana, veterinary surgeon
Zelimir Cernelic (1949), photographer
Jadranko Dumancic (1952), Zagreb, marine engineer
Srecko Favro (1971), Split, information scientist
Dinko Filipovic (1954), Virovitica, mechanical engineer
Branimir Gjetvaj (1960), Zagreb, Halifax, biologist
Mladen Gomercic (1966), Zagreb, mechanical engineer
Nikola Holjevac (1955), Slunj, mechanical engineer
Branimir Horvatin (1942), Zapresic, carpenter
Drago Ipsa (1948), Zagreb, geologist
Klement Jadresic (1972), Split, engineering student
Nenad Junek (1950), Zagreb, electrician
Krizo Katinic (1952), Kricanovo, physician
Dusko Kotlar (1974), Slavonski Brod, student
Kruno Kovacevic (1959), Virovitica, economist
Luka Loncarevic (1971), Zadar, medical student
Zeljko Ostruznjak (1955), Zagreb, construction technician
Boris Palaversic (1954), Zagreb, mechanical engineer
Srecko Radojkovic (1956), Zagreb, economist
Tomislav Resetar (1943), Karlovac, technician
Norberto Rodriguez (1933), Punta Arenas, officer
Bor Sotlar (1956), Ljubljana, economist
Drago Stimac (1952), Virovitica, engineering technician
Mihajlo Strelec (1958), Zagreb, physician
Dino Tadic (1973), Split, seamanship student
Branko Tomasic (1951), Virovitica, electrical engineer
Srecko Trajbar (1971), Zagreb, science student
Berislav Vahcic (1968), Zagreb, mechanical engineer
Jasminka Vicenski (1971), Zagreb, student
Nenad Vlahovic (1959), Gotaldovo, mechanical engineer

STAGES OF THE VOYAGE

1994

Kraljevica to Lisbon

Mladen Sutej, Dubravko Belan, Miro Muhek, Tatjana Tetus-Sutej, Alan Smojver, Tomislav Resetar; Krizo Katinic joined on Mallorca.

Lisbon to Newfoundland to Greenland to Lunenburg

Mladen, Belan, Miro, Tatjana, Jelena Belamaric, Srecko Trajbar, Nenad Junek; Branimir Gjetvaj joined us in St. John's.
Total: 8,322 miles sailed.

1995

Lunenburg to Northwest Passage to Vancouver

Mladen Sutej, Miro Muhek, Igor Milkovic, Srecko Trajbar, Nenad Junek and Drago Ipsa. In Nome, Trajbar suddenly left the ship, and in short order I called up Zeljko Ostruznjak, asking him to come to Dutch Harbor, so that the four of us should not have to sail, tired as we were, across the stormy north Pacific.
In 1995 *Cigra*'s log registered 8,100 miles.

1996

After work was completed in the TOM-MAC shipyard and the boat had been prepared for the rest of the voyage, I had to return to Zagreb. Miro Muhek took over the command of Cigra and calmly, routinely, sailed her to Los Angeles (San Pedro). In his crew were Drago Stimac, Dinko Filipovic, Mladen Gomercic, Srecko Radojkovic, Zelimir Cernelic and Branko Tomasic.

In Los Angeles, according to plan, Tomasic left Cigra and I came back on board.

In Cabo San Lucas, Baja California, everyone except Miro and I left the ship. The team that had the task of mastering the greater part of the Pacific, crossing the Equator and arriving in Polynesia included Jelena Belamaric, Dino Tadic and Nenad Vlahovic. The sixth member of the crew sent me a fax in Cabo: "Injured my leg playing tennis yesterday. Achilles tendon. Can't come." . . . Amusing.

Vancouver to Cabo San Lucas: 2010 miles

On Nuku Hiva, Jelena left to explore the Polynesian seabed, and my wife, Tanja, appeared, with a twelve-month-old bundle, Ana. We managed to sail together for a month. Ana practiced her first steps on a floor that was constantly slanting, while her mother worried, and the crew showed a high degree of resistance to tears, to waking at night and handling everything that is hard enough to organize at home, let alone on board.

Cabo San Lucas to Tahiti: 4,101 miles.

Air France brought new players to Tahiti: Branimir Horvatin, Boris Palavrsic, Kruno Kovacevic and Luka Loncarevic. Some of them arrived without luggage or wine from home, which had stayed behind in Paris. We found the loss of the wine the hardest to forgive. Tanja and Ana left, flying home via Tokyo, because there were no seats remaining for Europe. Nenad flew to Paris after a few days of waiting, and Dino, feeling completely at home on Cigra, *went on with us.*

On Robinson Crusoe Island the crew was beefed up by Jadranko Dumancic and Nikola Holjevac. Miro and I saw them all off later at the airport in Santiago.

Tahiti – Valparaiso: 4,527 miles

To prevent us from having to drive twice from Valparaiso to the airport, we arranged it so the recruits arrived on the same plane on which the old hands flew home. Alan Smovjer returned to Cigra, *with Bor Sotlar, Berislav Vahcic, Jasminka Vicenski and Miso Strelec. We picked up the eighth member of the crew, Damjan Brajnika, a few days later in Valdivia. This was a happy moment for me, because I handed the camera to him, and from then on the expedition was filmed properly. Apart from cooking and taking the helm, I freed him of all other duties.*

In Punta Arena, Norberto Rodriguez brought his gear on board, which increased the crew to nine for our voyage to Antarctica. Norberto flew home from the Falklands on DAP Airlines, one of the two airlines that link Tierra del Fuego and the Falklands with the world. (The RAF flies to

Stanley from a base near London; DAP, owned by Señor Pivcevic of Punta
Arenas, flies twice a week from there.)
Valparaiso to Antarctica to Buenos Aires: 4,592 miles.

1997—The last leg of the expedition [not covered in this book]

It was mainly students that flew into Buenos Aires. Joining us were Dino
Tadic and Luka Loncarevic, as well as Dusko Kotlar, Klement Jadresic and
Srecko Favro.

Financial problems of the expedition forced me to leave Cigra in Rio de
Janeiro, and Miro once again took over the thankless task of taking command, and having the lives of a young crew in his hands.

Igor Milkovic, Krizo Katinic and I joined the boat once again on Gran
Canaria. After a few days we said goodbye to Krizo on Madeira, and the
crew that carried on to the end was reinforced in Malta by Drago Stimac.

The circumnavigation of the globe was completed at Gibraltar on May 22,
1997, and we sailed back into Kraljevica on June 8, 1997, to a welcome
excellently organized by the people of this town we hold so dear.
Accompanied by numerous dinghies and yachts, and carefully looked after
by the port and municipal authorities who did everything to make our
arrival as simple and peaceful as possible, we tied up in the same spot,
touching the quay with the same side, from which we had set out on an
uncertain voyage some 37 months earlier.
Buenos Aires to Kraljevica: 8375 miles.

All told, in sailing around the world, we traveled 40,027 miles.

We motored for 5,920 miles (4,040 in the Arctic labyrinth) and were
under sail for 34,107. The 14 percent of the voyage during which we used
the motor was an inescapable necessity. We might have been able to sail a
few more miles, but we were often tied to airline schedules and crew
changes. Circumnavigating the globe using routes as exacting as these and
yet arriving on time for every single crew change was additional proof of a
job well done.

CIGRA'S DESIGN

The basic plans for *Cigra* were designed by Bruce Roberts, an American marine architect firm that has created plans for over 4000 boats now sailing the seas of the world. The model, originally known as the Trader 65, is the largest yacht designed by this firm. We did not depart from the architect's basic designs for the hull and rigging because I believed he understood these two things better than we did; I felt that any departure from his original ideas would upset the overall design. However, everything else on *Cigra* is different.

In the Kraljevica Shipyard during our first conversations, the builders proposed using nionicral—better quality plating than is normally used in shipbuilding. The making of the longitudinal frames with Holland sections—also of nionicral—is a different welding technology, characteristic of a military shipyard and technologically years ahead of civil yards.

Since we had paid only $900 for the plans to build the boat, it was clear to everyone how much we got for our money. Other than the hull, we completed everything ourselves. The ideas and the drawings developed during the construction drove the shipyard experts and engineers to distraction, as it did the inspectors of the Croatian Shipping Register. We owe them special recognition for their patience and tact

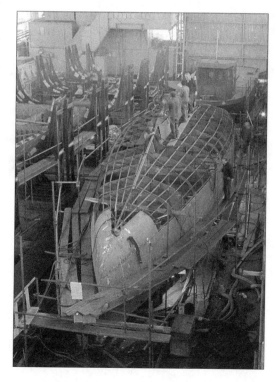

while they worked with a determined group of sailing enthusiasts.

When construction began, only about a dozen people believed that a boat would come out of this one day; less than that thought it would eventually sail the seas. But as the hull grew to completion, there was more enthusiasm, and more people began to believe in us. By the end, about 700 people had taken part in our project, all of them making tangible contributions. It proved that, despite the war (1993), the extremely difficult economic conditions, and the strange surroundings we were living in, we could achieve first-class results—a completely unexpected plus.

Cigra was launched precisely 10 months and three days after the signing of the contract with the shipyard (the first in the country after Croatia became independent). This was our first victory. *Vessel 501*, as it was officially called, was christened by a twelve year old girl, Nina Sirola: "Proud ship, I give you the name *Hrvatska Cigra (Croatian Tern)*. At that moment we were unable to control ourselves, and there were lots of hugs and occasional tears of joy.

TECHNICAL DATA

Length of hull, not including
bowsprit   19.80 m (65 ft.)
Length overall   22.44 m (74 ft.)
Length at the waterline   17.90 m
(59 ft.)
Beam   5.06 m (17 ft.)
Draft   1.83 m (6 ft.)
Displacement   47 tons
Ballast   12 tons

Plating thickness
Hull above water   5 mm
Hull in bow zone   7 mm
Ice breaking ram   7 mm
Hull below the waterline   6 mm
Hull in the keel   6 mm
Deck   4 mm
Superstructure (aluminum)   5 mm

Engine, Detroit Diesel, 6 cylinders
in line, two stroke, two circulation
cooling system, hydraulic transmission, 171 kW (230 HP)

Auxiliary Engine and generator:
Peugeot 30 kW and TESU 15 kW
generator

Fuel storage: 13 separate tanks and
one day-tank linked by a piping system; three pumps that make any
tanking system possible; total storage capacity 2600 liters.

Water: two 550 liter, stainless steel
tanks with foot-operated membrane
water pumps.

Rigging
Height of the main mast   19.2 m
(63 ft.)
Height of the mizzen mast 17.17 m
(56 ft.)
Shrouds (steel-steel, pre-stressed) 12
and 14 mm

Sails	m2	g/m2
main (Dacron)	72	500
mizzen (Dacron)	38	400
folding Genoa (Dacron)	82	250
folding jib (Dacron)	30	350
Genakker (nylon)	199	48

Speed
engine (1800 rpm)   9-10 knots
working (1400 rpm)   7 knots
under sail   12 knots

Other Equipment
Anchor CQR 90 kg	1
Anchor BRUCE 50 kg	1
Chain 16 mm, 100 m	2
Auxiliary boat RIS	1
Outboard motor MERCURY 20 HP	1
POLARIS motorized hang-glider	1
Desalinator	1
Rectifier and charger	2
Anemometer	1

Generator for engine shaft	1	**Communications Equipment**	
Various pumps	16	VHF SHIPMATE	1
Batteries (in sets of four)	12	VHF YEASU	1
Fire extinguisher for		VHF with handset	3
engine room, with warning	1	HF KENWOOD	1
		HF YEASU	1
Heating		HF ICOM M	1
WEBASTO central heating		Pactor modem	1
REFLEX diesel heater in the salon		PC laptop	1
Heat exchanger in the engine room			

Navigational Equipment
Compass by KOMPAS, Rijeka 1
GPS by TRIMBLE 2
Log and knotmeter, B & G 1
Wind speed and direction B & G 2
Sextant, PLATH 1
Radar, FURUNO 1
Depth meter, FURUNO 1
Weatherfax, FURUNO 1

White polyurethane foam for insulation was applied after we had installed and checked all the installations.

Detail of the welding of the Holland section longitudinal frames with watertight bulkheads

Enjoy these other adventure books from FineEdge.com

Arctic Odyssey
Len Sherman
The account of *Dove III*'s epic voyage through the Northwest Passage—one of the first west-to-east single-year passages on record.

Cape Horn
One Man's Dream, One Woman's Nightmare
Réanne Hemingway-Douglass
"This is the sea story to read if you read only one."
—McGraw Hill, Interntl. Marine Catalog

Trekka Round the World
John Guzzwell
"John Guzzwell is an inspiration to all blue-water sailors."—*Wooden Boat*
"A classic of small boat voyaging."—*Pacific Yachting*

Final Voyage of the *Princess Sophia*
Did they all have to die?
Betty O'Keefe and Ian Macdonald
This story explores the heroic efforts of those who answered the SOS, at first to save and later to recover the bodies of those lost.

Sea Stories of the Inside Passage
Iain Lawrence
"I can't wait to read Iain's next sea story; he describes the life of the Inside Passage like no one else."
—Sherrill and Rene Kitson, Ivory Island Lightstation

Exploring Southeast Alaska
Dixon Entrance to Skagway
Don Douglass and Réanne Hemingway-Douglass
Over 1500 anchor sites in Alaska's breathtaking southeastern archipelago; for pleasurable cruising to thousands of islands and islets, deeply-cut fjords, tidewater glaciers and icebergs.

Exploring Vancouver Island's West Coast—*Second Edition*
Don Douglass and Réanne Hemingway-Douglass
With five great sounds, sixteen major inlets, and an abundance of spectacular wildlife, the largest island on the west coast of North America is a cruising paradise.